2000

# THE Billboard BOOK OF

# SONG
# *writing*

## Peter Pickow and Amy Appleby

A Blue Cliff Editions Book

BILLBOARD PUBLICATIONS, INC. / NEW YORK

Blue Cliff Editions has conducted an exhaustive search to locate the composers, publishers, or copyright owners of the compositions in this book. However, in the event that we have inadvertently published a previously copyrighted composition without proper acknowledgement, we advise the copyright owner to contact us so that we may give appropriate credit in future editions.

Managing Editor:  Jackie Ogburn
Interior Design:  Margo Dittmer
Typesetting:  JetSet Typography

Library of Congress Cataloging-in-Publication Data

Pickow, Peter
     The Billboard book of songwriting / by Peter Pickow.
        p.  cm.
     "A Blue Cliff editions book."
     Bibliography: p.
     Includes index.
     ISBN 0-8230-7539-7
     1. Popular music—Writing and publishing.  2. Music trade.  I. Billboard.  II. Title  III. Title: Billboard book of song writing.   IV. Title: Book of songwriting.   V. Title: Book of song writing.
MT67.P5 1988
784.5'0026—dc19

ISBN 0-8230-7539-7

Manufactured in the United States of America

First printing, 1988

1  2  3  4  5  6  7  8  9/93  92  91  90  89  88

# Permissions

*To our mothers*


## Acknowledgments

Many thanks to Jason Shulman, Jackie Ogburn, Melinda Corey, and Julie Polkes for their unswerving dedication and creative direction. Special thanks to Sam Austin and Rob La Rocco for their excellent advice and to Curtis Cates of Big Iron for his humor and inspiration.

# Contents

# Introduction

Throughout history, people have used song to communicate emotions and ideas. Songwriters in ancient times used songs to express their understanding and awe of nature and the supernatural. Through music, people attempted to control the natural environment, to touch the supernatural world, and to explain the unknown. History and religion were recorded and preserved in the myths and legends expressed in song.

To this day, we turn to song to portray the struggles and joys of human existence. Thus, the songwriter provides a way for diverse peoples to share important ideas and emotions. The universal power of music is so strong that the work of a truly great songwriter may sometimes seem to penetrate all cultural boundaries. Benny Goodman described this phenomenon well: "Perhaps music will help all people to listen and think together. . . . I would like to think that while some people break the sound barrier, some of the rest of us break through other barriers with the sound of music."

Although most songwriters would like their music to reach as many people as possible, a song is often first aimed at a particular cross-section, such as pop, rock, or jazz listeners. In most cases, the commercial success of a song depends on its ability to be classified as a particular musical style. For this reason, it is important that a songwriter be aware of who's out there listening, and how to target song material for a particular audience.

More than 125,000 songs are registered for copyright in Washington, D.C., annually and hundreds of thousands more are written each year that go unregistered. The people who write all these songs have many different purposes in mind, and they measure their success in different ways. Commercial success is one important reason to write songs, but many successful songs are not necessarily written to compete on the charts. The writers of the earliest blues and rockabilly songs, for example, were not expecting commercial success from their creations; they focused their attention and effort only on the making of music.

Today there is a broad spectrum of possibilities for the talented songwriter, whether amateur, semipro, or professional. A song might be written as material for a college rock band or as the next Springsteen classic. Perhaps a writer needs a theme song for a community fund-raising event or an anthem for a charity effort on the global scale of "We Are the World." A grade-school teacher might write a song to help the class learn multiplication or a song might be conceived as a fun teaching tool for millions of *Sesame Street* viewers. You may want to write a song as a tribute to a friend or because you are under contract to write the theme song of a major motion picture. No matter what kind of songwriter you are or what type of songs you write, the rules and standards of the creative process are basically the same. That's why the lifespan of a great song can last for generations as it is adapted and readapted to the popular styles of the day.

Being a great songwriter is one thing, but understanding the various media in which your songs may be heard and getting to know your listener are also important. It is in this spirit that this book is offered. As you go through it you will notice that we have tried to look at the songwriting process from both the commercial and the aesthetic viewpoints (which are not all that different). But if you are serious about songwriting, you have to get serious about your expectations. The techniques and information that follow will help you hone your skills to the point where you will be able to write a good song and recognize what makes it good. Where you take it from there depends on your own vision and goals.

## How to Use This Book

There are many books on songwriting available today that focus on selling your songs. Although this book will give you some help with copyrighting your material, it is designed as a guide to the fundamentals of music and lyric writing and as a resource of songwriting techniques and ideas. The only sure way to maximize your potential as a songwriter is to learn as much as you can about the nuts and bolts of a well-crafted song and let your talent take it from there.

Most successful songwriters will tell you that the creative method they use differs from song to song. Because songwriting method is so much a factor of individual style and creativity, there is no cut-and-dried way to learn to write a good song.

The chapters that follow will help you identify your strengths and goals as a songwriter. This should cue you in to which chapters of the book you will want to spend the most time with and help you choose the method of songwriting that works best for you. You will also find an overview of the essential tools of the trade and how to use them to your best advantage. The final chapters provide a survey of today's popular styles and tips on how to make a song work well in each category, be it pop, rock, jazz, country, blues, or rhythm and blues (R&B). Naturally, you'll be drawn to the chapters dealing with techniques and styles of music that are already familiar to you. But it's a good idea to work through the other chapters as well, to broaden your horizons, spark your creativity, and add to your bag of songwriting tricks.

# You, the Songwriter

*Songwriting, like any other sport, demands that you stay in shape. And to stay in shape, what I do is I try to write between twenty-five and thirty songs a day. Now, you're right to chuckle. Really, out of that, of course a few are going to be losers, but you'd be surprised how many are very good.*

—*Martin Mull*
Comedian, songwriter

Whether you are writing songs for pleasure, profit, or both, your goal is to write better and better songs. The way to do this is to learn more about your craft through reading about and listening to the great songs of yesterday and today, and by writing, writing, writing, and then writing some more. Whether your taste runs to the music of Irving Berlin, Merle Haggard, or David Bowie, the songwriters you admire had to throw away at least ten unfinished or flawed song ideas for every song completed.

The more songs you write, and the closer you get to your own style of songwriting, the more you need to know about the methods and styles of other songwriters. If you like country music, you can learn a lot from the blues, and any writer of rock songs who doesn't know his blues and country is talking through his hat. Many of the great innovators drew their inspiration from a combination of musical styles. And if you don't think versatility pays off, talk to Roger Miller, writer of the country hit "King of the Road," pop hit "England Swings," and the Tony-award-winning score to the Broadway musical *Big River*. Or ask James Taylor if he minded when Elvis Presley did the chart-topping rock and roll version of "Steamroller Blues." Taking what you need from the various styles of popular music is a sure way to develop your own unique style and to make sure that it will reach its largest audience. As veteran songwriter and performer Ray Charles explains, "I only began to get real recognition . . . when I started to mix pop with my blues-and-jazz style. I wanted to show the pop people that you don't have to conform to those rock 'n' roll sounds. I didn't want to follow others. I wanted to innovate."

You know that you want to create songs that are fresh and innovative, but keep in mind that the marketability and performance potential of your songs depend on their being identified with a particular style or genre, whether it be rock, pop, country, jazz, blues, rhythm and blues, gospel, or soul. Yet within the boundaries of each of these, there is plenty of room to stretch out.

## What Kind of Songwriter Are You?

Songwriters come from a variety of musical backgrounds, but we all have one thing in common: a love of and interest in popular song. Maybe you play a solo instrument or play and sing with a band. Perhaps you are primarily a vocalist or do a solo act accompanying yourself on an instrument. You may be a lyricist with a good sense of song form and of how it affects a song's melody and words. Because songwriters hail from such a wide range of musical backgrounds, many different approaches are popularly used for writing songs. Some songs start out as just a guitar riff or as a chord progression pounded out on an out-of-tune upright piano. Other songs are created lyrics first, as a few words set to a melody hummed in the shower or as nothing more than a catchy title. Whatever your musical background you will need a good grasp of all aspects of the craft. In this way, you can use your talents to the fullest and most effectively communicate your musical ideas to producers, performers, and audiences.

In the same way that a jazz dancer, a modern dancer, and a ballet dancer each bring different strengths to their chosen style of dance, so different kinds of songwriters develop different skills. A pop or jazz writer might be more adept at inventing harmony than someone who writes music that is harmonically less demanding, like country or blues. But a blues or country writer might be an expert at creating melody or lyric or at giving a song a solid structure. A songwriter who writes rock or rhythm and blues usually has a highly developed sense of rhythm, but might need to work on matching the music with meaningful lyrics.

You already know what kind of musical styles you prefer and have done quite a bit of listening, performing, or writing within these genres. It's a good idea to be aware of the particular talents that you bring to songwriting and how you can grow by exploring the areas you are less familiar with.

### The Instrumentalist as Songwriter

Many songwriters are instrumentalists who have learned to apply their playing talents to writing their own material. Peter Townshend of the Who is equally admired for his guitar pyrotechnics and his songwriting. Part of his success as a rock songwriter is grounded in his guitar style and the way he incorporates it in his songs. Consider Mose Allison, the jazz piano player who writes sometimes witty, sometimes introspective, always clever songs, such as "Your Mind Is on Vacation and Your Mouth Is Working Overtime." Both in the writing and in the delivery of his material, his piano style is an important element.

Instrumentalists are usually well aware of the power of melody and phrasing. If you're a guitarist or a keyboardist, you are probably skilled at harmonizing and arranging songs. Guitarists, pianists, bass players, and drummers also have a natural ability to create rhythm in their songs and are often able to add a catchy groove or feeling to their work. The blues great John Lee Hooker put it this way: "If I get an idea I'll think about it and get it together and then I'll pick up a guitar and phrase it. I'll play it once to get the sound, the feeling, the beat."

If you are an instrumentalist, chances are you usually come up with the melody, harmony, or groove of a song first and add the words as a last step, often in collaboration with a lyricist. Keith Richard of the Rolling Stones sums it up: "I can write a song out of a chord sequence, a riff, and eventually come up with lyrics to fit onto it, but the other way around, no way." Although you may use this same approach to songwriting, you might still want to try writing the lyrics first. Sometimes breaking your pattern with a new approach can bring fresh insights and add more depth to your songwriting style.

### The Singer as Songwriter

A singer is naturally aware of the power of melody and lyric. Songwriters like Cyndi Lauper and Stevie Wonder, who first earned fame as performers, have effectively directed their songwriting talents toward writing good material for themselves. This kind of songwriter generally comes up with one or both of these elements first and then seeks collaborators to help create the harmony and instrumentation for the song. If you are a singer, this lyric/melody-first approach can be very effective: who better than a singer can understand the capabilities, strengths, and weaknesses of the human voice?

As a performer, the singer has first-hand experience at putting across song lyrics and understanding the importance of a strong theme and situation, the clear voice of the speaker, and the development of interesting characters and events. Still, many successful singers and instrumentalists stick to writing the music and collaborate with lyricists on their songs. Speech patterns, sounds, and the mechanics of singing them are the singer's stock-in-trade. A songwriter with this background is especially aware of the importance of a good marriage of melody and lyrics and the benefits of natural and distinctive rhythms. If you are a singer/songwriter, you might want to learn more about song harmony and arrangement. You may currently do your songwriting "by ear" and could benefit a lot by learning a little about music theory and notation. Chances are your songwriting ability will also profit from talking to instrumentalists about song performance and interpretation.

### The Lyricist

Although all lyricists understand the way a song works, and how music affects language and vice versa, a lyricist need not be a musician. Many great songwriting teams in popular music history have preferred a strict division of labor between composer and lyricist. These include such great partnerships as Rodgers and Hart, Webber and Rice, and Elton John and Bernie Taupin. Although the lyricist is usually not greatly involved in the creation of the musical elements of a song, he or she is certainly familiar with rhythmic and melodic effects, for the lyricist must work most closely with these aspects of the song.

Many lyricists first learned about using language with meter, rhyme, and imagery by writing poetry. When they began writing song lyrics, they soon learned the important similarities and differences between poetry and song lyrics. The main difference is that lyrics deal with the crucial marriage of words and music, while poetry, however "musical," deals with words alone. Lyricists who did not begin by writing poetry sometimes have an advantage over those who did, because music was always an integral part of their work.

Some songwriters compose both the music and lyrics of their songs, and many successful songs have been entirely written by one person. If you are both composer and lyricist, then you are experienced with the process of matching a song's words and music in the fullest sense. You not need rely on collaborators to complete a song, although you might use an arranger to help with the song's instrumentation. Some songwriters handle their own arrangements.

If you are a lyricist, pure and simple, you are going to need a collaborator to finish your song, so you would probably benefit from talking with melodists and composers about how they work. This way, you can make the collaborative approach to songwriting as productive and smooth as possible.

### The Composer or Melodist

In this category fall those writers who concentrate on writing the music. There is understandably a bit of overlap with the instrumentalists, since few songwriters compose in a vacuum, but often there is a clear distinction between instrumentalist/songwriters and the popular song composer. On the one hand, there are the instrumentalists like Duke Ellington, who wrote hundreds of well-known songs, but was also famous as a bandleader and an innovator in jazz arranging. On the other hand, many great composer/songwriters, like George Gershwin, Richard Rodgers, and many of the Tin Pan Alley and musical comedy composers, were not professional performers.

Usually composers have a working knowledge of guitar or piano or of band conducting or arranging. These media all offer the composer the opportunity to become familiar with harmony, music theory, and notation. Many composers do not write their own lyrics and require a collaborator to complete a song. With this in mind, it is a good idea to talk to lyricists about their working methods, so you can make your own collaborations as fruitful as possible.

## Your Goals as a Songwriter

Your main goal as a songwriter is to keep writing good songs and the best way to accomplish this is to play or listen to good music and to incorporate aspects you like into your own originals. You want to absorb all this input and apply it to your own material in a creative and original way. (To this end, it's important to be aware of the fine line between a song idea that is fair to borrow and protected song material. Refer to "Copyright Basics" in the Appendix for guidelines.)

There are many aspects to creating and promoting a song, from arranging a demo session to straightening your files of song ideas. Some songwriters get so busy with "the business of music" that they lose sight of the fact that their job is to write good songs. Naturally, a song doesn't get out there and promote itself, so you do need to get it heard and played. But don't get too hung up on all the trappings of making it in the business, or you'll have no time to create what's most important—a superb song.

### Writing Songs to Perform Yourself

Since songwriters come from different musical backgrounds, sometimes their immediate goals also vary greatly. For instance, a singer/guitarist like James Taylor writes songs to perform himself. Although Yes's guitarist and songwriter Steve Howe doesn't generally sing his own songs, he plays on every recording. The list of songwriters who perform their own material professionally is endless. Some notable writers of this kind include Willie Nelson, Joni Mitchell, Randy Newman, B.B. King, Frank Zappa, Mick Jagger, Carole King, Cyndi Lauper, and Prince.

Some writers may intend a song for another artist and find that it ends up being a great song to perform themselves. Carole King says of this approach,

"Most of the songs I write for any other artist I can sing. I could be thinking of another artist completely, but since I'm the one writing it and I'm the one who has to sing it to convey it to the artist, ultimately I wind up singing it in one way or another, and by the time I've sung it for demonstration purposes, it has become mine."

Writing a song with another performer in mind might be an approach to help you distance yourself a little from your material. It is important for the style and range of the song to be well-suited to your abilities as a performer, but usually you don't want to make it impossible for another artist to perform, for this may reduce its commercial value. Although your goal is to write songs for yourself, you want to be sure that their value is enhanced by, but not dependent on, your performance. No matter who it is intended for, a good song should be able to stand on its own.

### Writing for Other Artists

Though it has become increasingly popular in recent years for songwriters to perform their own work, there are many successful songwriters who do not sing or play an instrument professionally. Instead, they write songs exclusively for other performers. Many of the great songwriting success stories involved this kind of songwriter—from Cole Porter and Richard Rodgers to Lieber and Stoller (who wrote many of Elvis Presley's hits) and Burt Bacharach.

Some people become performing artists after they are well-established as songwriters. Often this is prompted by the writer's desire to express important nuances of a song in his or her own style. Willie Nelson, Neil Diamond, and Lionel Richie were well-known songwriters before they became recording artists. Whether performing your own material is in your future or not, if you are writing songs for another artist, it helps to know the style and tone you want for the piece and to be able to communicate this feeling to a vocalist or musician.

Many times, songwriters do not know who will be performing their songs. The material of many singer/songwriters, originally intended for themselves, sometimes ends up being more successful in the hands of another recording artist. Dolly Parton's song "Kentucky Gambler" was not a big hit for her, but had considerable success in the Merle Haggard version. The Platters made a number one hit of Otto Harbach and Jerome Kern's "Smoke Gets in Your Eyes," which was first heard in their Broadway production of the musical *Roberta*. So you can see why it's sometimes hard to predict which artists will do best with a given song.

When writing songs for other artists to perform, it can be inspiring to have a specific person or group in mind. You may be writing song material for a performer or band that you know personally or for a particular recording artist or band you admire. If so, you probably know what style of song you're writing before you even begin. If you have a specific singer in mind when you sit down to write a song, you know the general range and character of the melody as limited by the abilities of the vocalist. If you are writing for a specific instrumentalist or band, you will also have some ideas about the song's instrumentation. Having all this information can be helpful in the early stages of the writing process and it can provide a focus for your creative powers.

It pays to keep in mind that a song's commercial value depends on its ability to stand on its own merits without the help of heavy instrumentation or stylized performance techniques. For example, although it will help you in the promotion stage to have a demo of your song, the rendition you choose should not include a lot of special effects and styling or rely heavily on the talents of a particular singer or instrumentalist to get it across. A clear and straightforward rendition of your song will sound much more professional and polished. So when you are writing a song with a specific artist or band in mind, be sure that the success of the song does not rely heavily on performance factors. It may be recorded by someone entirely different from the person you had in mind when you wrote it.

### Making Songwriting Your Business

A good song should speak for itself; it will never become an industry hit if you don't get it heard by people in the music business. For many songwriters, commercial success is an important goal; and if this is true for you, you'll want to be familiar with the business aspects of songwriting. These include getting your song copyrighted and making a quality demo.

Today's songwriter has many avenues for the production and performance of song material. Records and tapes, as well as CDs and video are the recording industry's stock-in-trade. The broadcasting industry—with radio and network and cable television—provides another major arena for songs. There is considerable demand for song material in the movie industry and on Broadway. There's also the music publishing industry, which usually produces songs in written form—sheet music and songbooks. And, there is an ever-increasing need for songs in education and business and even in the government. Finally, there is the world of advertising, which supports the many songwriters who create jingles and commercial song themes. Because the basic forms and themes of jingles are quite different from almost every other type of popular song today, jingle-writing falls outside the subject area of this book, which focuses only on the characteristics of a good song and how to improve your ability to write one.

# What Makes a Great Song?

*If I'm satisfied [with a song] I know it's finished. And I always know if it's good. But whether it's great, you only know that in terms of external acknowledgement, acceptance, because after all, one of the things we're trying to do is write songs that will be appreciated on all different kinds of levels.*

—*Doc Pomus*

You have probably listened to thousands of songs in your lifetime and are a good judge of what works and what doesn't. If a song is popular (if it does well on the *Billboard* charts), chances are it is pretty good. Although you can surely name a few not-so-great songs that did well on the charts, for the most part, the public recognizes a good song when they hear it.

You want to write good songs, but you also want to get them heard by the people whose business it is to get songs performed and recorded. It's important to know your market and to be familiar with the current trends in the types of music you write, but take care not to get sidetracked thinking too much about flashy extras to sell your song. Your final product should be as good as you can make it, but as a songwriter your most important work is done at the beginning. Great arrangements and production values mean nothing without a solid song for them to work their magic on.

The truly great songs are released, make a hit, and never really go away. Prewar classics like "Puttin' on the Ritz" and "What'll I Do?" have enjoyed countless revivals, spanning decades. Surely many Beatles and Stevie Wonder songs will be performed as classics in the twenty-first century.

Look at any of the classic songs of our time and you will notice they all have one thing in common: melody, harmony, and lyric work together to create a memorable statement or mood. The theme of the lyric is almost always universal and timeless—love, joy, desperation, patriotism. Many great songs express universal themes using personal references and meaningful details. A perfect example is "A Foggy Day" by George and Ira Gershwin. The song's lyric, melody, and harmony work together beautifully to evoke the time, place, and mood of a personal romantic remembrance. Because the lyricist has chosen familiar images, we are able to share this feeling of longing and love.

Some songs achieve classic status because of their powerful moral message and well-constructed "raw edge." In Stevie Wonder's lyrics to "Superstition," melody works with rhythm and riffs to create a riveting warning to the common man to break the chains of ignorance and fear of the unknown. Bob Dylan and Pete Seeger practically founded their careers on writing and performing songs that contain powerful social messages like "Blowin' in the Wind" and "Where Have All the Flowers Gone." Some great pop songs use social and political themes. Think of Pink Floyd's "Money" or the great rock operas *Tommy* and *Jesus Christ Superstar.*

Even though sometimes a song may be remembered for a particularly striking lyric, or a great theme or melody, it is very rare that a song is successful because of only one of these elements. You may know of songs whose success seems to be attributable to their great lyrics but on closer examination you will probably find that the simplicity of their melodies is by no means a weakness. It serves to support and enhance the prominent lyrics. For example, the melody and harmony of Bob Dylan's "Blowin' in the Wind" is quite simple and repetitive. The folksy simplicity of the melody and harmony point up the chilling antiwar message of the lyric.

"Ode to Billie Joe" has an extremely repetitive melody which might, at first glance, seem quite weak in view of the heavily expressive lyric. But this simple melody (which, taken alone, could be said to verge on the inane) provides the transparency necessary to let the desperate situation described in the lyric make its powerful impact. As the tense, dramatic situation unfolds, the melody's simplistic qualities underscore the hypnotic and ultimately chilling narrative of a family's callous reaction to the young man's suicide.

Some songs' popularity results from their musical strength (melody, harmony, rhythm) rather than from notable lyrics. Often in these cases the secondary nature of the lyric is necessary to enhance a particularly lovely or clever melody, complex harmony, or striking rhythmic pattern or riff. For example, "Mood Indigo" by Duke Ellington has rich harmonic texture and an unusual, haunting melody. The lyrics are unobtrusive and focus on a single theme—being blue.

> *You ain't been blue*
> *No, no, no.*
> *You ain't been blue,*

*Till you've had that mood indigo.*
*That feeling goes reeling*
*Down to my shoes*
*While I sit and sigh*
*Go 'long blues.*

First performed by the Ellington Band as an instrumental, the words were added as an afterthought. Because of the song's fame as an instrumental, the lyricist took care to make the words simple and unobtrusive, yet faithful to the melancholy mood of the music. Many other big band and jazz tunes are best known for their instrumental versions, with the lyrics an obvious afterthought.

As you can see, the trick to writing a great song lies in forging its various elements into a unified and pleasing whole. So, whatever features of the song you feel to be the strongest, whether it is the melody, harmony, rhythm, or lyric, be sure that all the other elements work to complement the things you like best. Just because you have a good lyric and a great tune does not mean that they will fit together well.

One of the major yardsticks of a song's success in the commercial market is its ability to reach many different types of listeners. "Crossover" is a hot word in songwriting today, because those songs that do cross over from one chart to another bring a wider audience and often considerable returns to the performers, producers, and songwriters involved. Dolly Parton can have a song that becomes a hit on the country, rock, and adult contemporary charts. With all the emphasis on Top 40 charts and the genres they try to define, it is easy to forget that many songs in the past achieved crossover status before there was ever a word for it. "My Favorite Things" started life as a sugary sweet number from *The Sound of Music* and then became popular as a landmark avant-garde jazz instrumental for John Coltrane. Or take "Blue Moon," by Rodgers and Hart, which started out as the third revision of a song originally written for movie star Jean Harlow and called "Make Me a Star" and "The Bad in Every Man." The song was so adaptable that it ended up, nearly thirty years after it was written, as a minor hit for Elvis Presley and a number one hit for the doo-wop group, the Marcels. While these are more properly examples of successful covers of songs rather than the crossover of a particular recorded version, they serve to lend some weight to the axiom that "a good song is a good song," and to illustrate that there is much to be learned from studying songs outside of your chosen genre.

# The Well-Organized Song

*The songwriting process, as I know it, is one of almost a conveyer belt system. I have maybe a dozen pieces of music all waiting for a verse or a chorus and they come off the conveyer belt at their own rate. I might have a verse or a chorus of a particular song, but I'm waiting for something to happen to me—so I can go, wow, I can use that right now. Then I get a pen and write it down.*

—Graham Nash

*Basically I just have a strong vision in my mind and I try to bring the song as close to that vision as I can. I have a love for simple, basic song structure, although sometimes you'd never know it.*

—Laura Nyro

No matter how tuneful the music or witty the lyrics, lack of structure or form in a song is a fatal flaw. In popular song, the term "form" refers to the pattern of a song's various sections, and the length and construction of the sections themselves. A good song is shaped and defined by its form, because form can affect every aspect of the song. Form is easy to overlook and an underdeveloped sense of form can be a severe limitation to any songwriter. If all your songs sound the same, it may be because you use the same form over and over. We have all heard songs that ramble or don't go anywhere. Either we lose interest after the first few moments or we get lost trying to follow them. These problems are often the result of the songwriter's lack of attention to appropriate song form. Good form is what holds a song together.

There are many standard song forms used in popular music today and many variations on each of them. As you explore the different song forms, by listening to music and using different forms in your own material, you will see that all songs have one thing in common. They all make use of distinct sections in contrasting and repeating patterns.

## Parts of a Song

Terms like "verse," "chorus," "bridge," and "release" are used loosely by songwriters and musicians. This can cause confusion and misunderstandings during collaboration or rehearsal. The following are general definitions of the parts of a song as they are most commonly used.

### Intro

Today's intro is usually a distinctive instrumental section at the beginning of the song, as in the gentle, ascending, augmented chords that open Stevie Wonder's "You Are the Sunshine of My Life" or the acoustic-guitar arpeggios at the top of Led Zeppelin's "Stairway to Heaven." You may also hear "oohs," "ahs," or humming from the lead or backup vocalists, as in Barbra Streisand's version of "The Way We Were," not to mention those doo-wop intros of the fifties, like "Blue Moon" by the Marcels or "Rama Lama Ding Dong," by the Edsels.

Older songs often included a fairly short, introductory section that set up the theme or subject matter of the song. Although usually referred to today as the "intro," it is more properly the song's "verse."

### The Verse

Although the term "verse" may refer to the introductory verse section of a song, most songwriters today use the term to mean the descriptive section of a song that comes before the chorus. Each verse of a song contains different lyrics, and it is here that the development of the story takes place. The verse is an integral part of the popular verse/chorus form and uses narrative and detail to set up the theme that is reflected upon in the chorus.

### The Chorus

The title or hook section of today's popular songs is repeated in the chorus, which usually follows the verse. Here the point of the song is made in its simplest terms and here, too, the songwriter has the best chance to make the most memorable statement. At one time the term "chorus" was used to refer to the main body of a song, while the term "verse" referred to the intro section at the beginning of a song. Our verse/chorus song form of today is actually an outgrowth of this older form.

### The Hook

The hook is an important phrase of the song, usually repeated or emphasized in the chorus. Sometimes it appears at the end of the verse and sometimes in both sections. The words to the hook, or part of the hook, often serve as the song's title, as in the Beatles' "Help," or Michael Jackson's "Beat It." For the hook to be easily recognizable, it often occurs at musical high points in the song.

### The Bridge

Many songs feature a section called a bridge instead of, or in addition to, the chorus. As its name implies, the bridge provides a transition between verses or, in some cases, from verse to chorus. Traditionally, the bridge section had a different function, as the contrasting eight-measure verse section in the verse/bridge song form. As such, it was an integral part of the chorus rather than a discrete section.

When writing the bridge of a song, keep in mind that its function is to provide a transition between verses. For this reason songwriters usually provide it with its own distinctive harmony and melody that lead nicely out of one verse and into another. Often the bridge's overall sense of contrast and movement is enhanced by a temporary change of key (modulation).

### The Coda

Many songs today feature a coda section at the end to further reinforce the hook or to express the theme or outcome of the lyric. Paul and Linda McCartney use a coda section at the end of "My Love," which reiterates the melody of the chorus. Irwin Levine and L. Russell Brown use a more traditional coda form at the end of "Say, Has Anybody Seen My Sweet Gypsy Rose." The basic tune of the last line of the chorus is repeated three times with a rhyme in each line: "Say has anybody seen *my,* now you know just what I mean *by,* has anybody seen *my* Gypsy Rose?" Many times the coda section is designed to fade out, as in the taglike coda at the end of Lennon and McCartney's "Hey Jude." Here the lyric is quite minimal, "da, da, da, da, da, da, da, da, da, da, da, Hey Jude," and this sequence is marked to "repeat and fade."

Remember that if you are using a coda or a tag that fades out, this is the last thing that the listener hears in your song. So, it's a good place to restate the hook/title and leave the listener with the important kernel of your song.

## Song Forms

To diagram the form of a song, musicians and writers often use a type of shorthand to describe the order of its large sections. For example, if A stands for a verse, B for a chorus, and C for the bridge, a typical pop song like "Lookin'

for Love" could be represented as ABABCBB as shown in this diagram using
the first line of each section.

*(Verse)* A:    *I spent a lot of time looking for love* . . . . . . . . . . . . . . . . . . . . . . . . .
. . . . . . . . . . . . . . . . . . . . . . . . . . . . . . . . . . . . . . . . . . . . . . . . . . . .
. . . . . . . . . . . . . . . . . . . . . . . . . . . . . . . . . . . . . . . . . . . . . . . . . . . .

*(Chorus)* B:    *Looking for love in all the wrong places* . . . . . . . . . . . . . . . . . . .
. . . . . . . . . . . . . . . . . . . . . . . . . . . . . . . . . . . . . . . . . . . . . . . . . . . .
. . . . . . . . . . . . . . . . . . . . . . . . . . . . . . . . . . . . . . . . . . . . . . . . . . . .
. . . . . . . . . . . . . . . . . . . . . . . . . . . . . . . . . . . . . . . . . . . . . . . . . . . .
. . . . . . . . . . . . . . . . . . . . . . . . . . . . . . . . . . . . . . . . . . . . . . . . . . . .
. . . . . . . . . . . . . . . . . . . . . . . . . . . . . . . . . . . . . . . . . . . . . . . . . . . .

*(Verse)* A:    *I was alone then, no love in sight* . . . . . . . . . . . . . . . . . . . . . . . . .
. . . . . . . . . . . . . . . . . . . . . . . . . . . . . . . . . . . . . . . . . . . . . . . . . . . .
. . . . . . . . . . . . . . . . . . . . . . . . . . . . . . . . . . . . . . . . . . . . . . . . . . . .

*(Chorus)* B:    *I was looking for love in all the wrong places* . . . . . . . . . . . . . .
. . . . . . . . . . . . . . . . . . . . . . . . . . . . . . . . . . . . . . . . . . . . . . . . . . . .
. . . . . . . . . . . . . . . . . . . . . . . . . . . . . . . . . . . . . . . . . . . . . . . . . . . .
. . . . . . . . . . . . . . . . . . . . . . . . . . . . . . . . . . . . . . . . . . . . . . . . . . . .
. . . . . . . . . . . . . . . . . . . . . . . . . . . . . . . . . . . . . . . . . . . . . . . . . . . .
. . . . . . . . . . . . . . . . . . . . . . . . . . . . . . . . . . . . . . . . . . . . . . . . . . . .

*(Bridge)* C:    *You came knocking at my heart's door* . . . . . . . . . . . . . . . . . . .
. . . . . . . . . . . . . . . . . . . . . . . . . . . . . . . . . . . . . . . . . . . . . . . . . . . .

*(Chorus)* B:    *No more looking for love in all the wrong places* . . . . . . . . . . . .
. . . . . . . . . . . . . . . . . . . . . . . . . . . . . . . . . . . . . . . . . . . . . . . . . . . .
. . . . . . . . . . . . . . . . . . . . . . . . . . . . . . . . . . . . . . . . . . . . . . . . . . . .
. . . . . . . . . . . . . . . . . . . . . . . . . . . . . . . . . . . . . . . . . . . . . . . . . . . .
. . . . . . . . . . . . . . . . . . . . . . . . . . . . . . . . . . . . . . . . . . . . . . . . . . . .
. . . . . . . . . . . . . . . . . . . . . . . . . . . . . . . . . . . . . . . . . . . . . . . . . . . .

*(Chorus)* B:    *Looking for love in all the wrong places* . . . . . . . . . . . . . . . . . . .
. . . . . . . . . . . . . . . . . . . . . . . . . . . . . . . . . . . . . . . . . . . . . . . . . . . .
. . . . . . . . . . . . . . . . . . . . . . . . . . . . . . . . . . . . . . . . . . . . . . . . . . . .
. . . . . . . . . . . . . . . . . . . . . . . . . . . . . . . . . . . . . . . . . . . . . . . . . . . .
. . . . . . . . . . . . . . . . . . . . . . . . . . . . . . . . . . . . . . . . . . . . . . . . . . . .
. . . . . . . . . . . . . . . . . . . . . . . . . . . . . . . . . . . . . . . . . . . . . . . . . . . .

Notice how the different sections of this song feature different lengths and
numbers of lines of lyric. The music also varies in each new section. Patterns
of repetition are central to good song form and, with rare exceptions, are the

one feature common to every successful song in the history of popular music. It pays to be able to construct good song forms and to identify the individual sections of your songs. It will make it much easier to talk with musicians, producers, or anyone else who is interested in discussing your work.

This nomenclature may be used to distinguish the basic sections of any song, including songs that use the more unified AABA form, like the classics "As Time Goes By" and "Blue Skies," and many of the hit songs by the Beatles. Here, the respective sections of the song are inextricably linked, and rely heavily upon one another to complete their sweeping AABA structure (or, more loosely, verse section/verse section/bridge/verse section.) The letters stand for the different types of sections in the song, so A could be an intro in one song and the verse in another. There are many variations on the AABA form, sometimes it is used with a coda section, or the final two sections are restated to form AABABA. Whatever the case, a true AABA form variant uses interdependent sections to create a whole and rarely features a chorus.

The other two basic song forms popular today are the AAA form and the verse/chorus form (normally, the verse and chorus sections of a verse/chorus song are not referred to as A and B.) The AAA song is simply verse/verse/verse, but there are variations (AA and even just A have worked too, and many AAA songs feature a decorative intro or coda). A more detailed discussion of these three basic forms, the AAA, the AABA, the verse/chorus form, appears in the sections that follow.

The benefits of using solid form and structure in your song are tremendous. The form of a song, more than any other feature, adds movement or, as they say in the business, it allows your song to build. No matter how distinctive the beat or how hot the riffs, your song will not communicate an overall sense of movement unless you have taken the time to give it a solid frame. The other important benefit gained from this kind of planning is the sense of polish and professionalism that good form will bring to your material. It is the hallmark of a true professional.

### The AAA Song Form—As It Was

The simplest, and perhaps oldest, song form still popular today is the AAA form. Traditionally, the musical structure of each section remains the same beneath the new lyric of each verse. The earliest English ballads use this form, because it is well-suited to the development of narrative. When used by songwriters today, its simple musical repetition of the verse often creates a tone of truthfulness and authority and can suggest a retrospective or old-fashioned feeling in a song. Paul Simon and Art Garfunkel used a traditional AAA-form folk tune, "Scarborough Fair," on their album of the same name.

> *(Verse) A:*      *Are you going to Scarborough Fair?*
>                    *Parsley, sage, rosemary, and thyme,*
>                    *Remember me to one who lives there,*
>                    *For she once was a true love of mine.*
> *(Verse) A:*      *Tell her to make me a cambric shirt,*
>                    *Parsley, sage, rosemary, and thyme,*
>                    *Without a stitch of needle work,*
>                    *Then she shall be a true love of mine.*

The form is quite simple and the lyrics are responsible for adding variation to the song. Classics that employ this form to tell an interesting story are "Frankie and Johnnie" and "Streets of Laredo," and many folk songs and hymns.

### The AAA Form Today

The AAA form need not always be folksy-sounding or nostalgic, although it never fails to communicate a feeling of simplicity or a romantic nod to the past. Some song successes that employ the basic AAA form include Bob Dylan's "Blowin' in the Wind" and Bobbie Gentry's "Ode to Billie Joe." More recently, there have been AAA hits like "The Rose" as recorded by Bette Midler and Roberta Flack's version of "The First Time Ever I Saw Your Face."

Sometimes the lyric simply repeats in each A section of the song, as in Stephen Schwartz's "Day by Day" from the musical *Godspell*. In some songs the A section is only repeated once or twice as in Chicago's memorable hit "Colour My World" by James Pankow, which is composed of one A section that is restated by the flute in the following instrumental. The very inventive and beautiful melody and lyric gives interest to the song's single section, which is framed with rich instrumentals. The hook is featured in the final line of the song.

Often the individual sections of this form may feature musical differences at the end of each verse or a coda or tag section to add a little variation to this simple form. Jim Webb's "By the Time I Get to Phoenix" uses two extra measures at the end of the second A section and a coda after the third section to add some dimension at the song's ending.

### The AABA Form—As It Was

During the heyday of Tin Pan Alley in the twenties and thirties, the most popular song form was AABA. In its strictest definition, the A sections and the B section are each eight measures long, making for a standard song length of thirty-two bars. All three As are musically identical to one another (perhaps with the exception of the last few notes to make for smoother transitions). The B is a contrasting section called the "bridge," or "release," which usually moves temporarily to a different key or through several keys before returning the song to the final restatement of the A. This entire section was known as the chorus and was preceded by an introductory section called the verse. Since the musical structure of the verse was often different from that of the main section of the song (the AABA part)—it could have a different key, time signature, or tempo—and since its lyric was often unimportant to the song as a whole, the verse was frequently omitted in performance. In big band arrangements, the verse was played as an instrumental introduction or interlude. In popular songs of today, this introductory verse section is almost universally viewed as an outmoded appendage.

There are many examples of the traditional AABA form with an introductory verse; in fact, many jazz standards follow this pattern. Just a few are: Jimmy McHugh's "On the Sunny Side of the Street," George Gershwin's "O! Lady Be Good" and "The Man I Love," and "Ain't Misbehavin' " by Fats Waller and Harry Brooks. Although frequently the introductory verse is not known, even to the best musicians, sometimes these sections are surprisingly pretty and can add freshness to the performance of an often-played standard.

After the introductory verse dropped away, the AABA form was left with what had been known collectively as the chorus, that is, the AABA part. This section is what most people think of as constituting songs like "Georgia on My Mind," "Smoke Gets in Your Eyes," and " 'S Wonderful," all of which were written with introductory verses that you rarely hear today.

### The AABA Form Today

The AABA form and its variants are still very popular today. Although the introductory verse section has almost vanished, the basic AABA form has changed very little. Although AABA form songs may be said to have verse sections and a bridge, all four of the AABA song's sections are more properly considered parts of a unified whole. Hits like James Pankow's "Just You 'n' Me" as recorded by Chicago or Hal David and Burt Bacharach's "(They Long to Be) Close to You" are clear renditions of the AABA form. Many Broadway tunes still favor the AABA form, as do the theme songs of movies, such as "(Where Do I Begin) Love Story" from the movie *Love Story* and "Memories," from the musical *Cats* by Andrew Lloyd Webber. Lennon and McCartney's "From Me to You," is another pure example of this form. Here, the contrasting B section is referred to as the bridge, and the repeated A sections may be referred to as the verses of the song.

*Verse: A:    If there's anything that you want . . . . . . . . . . . . . . . . . . . . . . . . . . . . . . . . . .*
. . . . . . . . . . . . . . . . . . . . . . . . . . . . . . . . . . . . . . . . . . . . . . . . . . . . . . . . . . . . . . .

> . . . . . . . . . . . . . . . . . . . . . . . . . . . . . . . . . . . . . .
> . . . . . . . . . . . . . . . . . . . . . . . . . . . . . . . . . . . . . .
> *Verse: A:*     *I've got everything that you want* . . . . . . . . . . . . . . . . . . . . . . . . . . .
> . . . . . . . . . . . . . . . . . . . . . . . . . . . . . . . . . . . . . .
> . . . . . . . . . . . . . . . . . . . . . . . . . . . . . . . . . . . . . .
> . . . . . . . . . . . . . . . . . . . . . . . . . . . . . . . . . . . . . .
> *Bridge: B:*        *I got arms that long to hold you* . . . . . . . . . . . . . . . . . . . . . .
> . . . . . . . . . . . . . . . . . . . . . . . . . . . . . . . . . . . . . .
> . . . . . . . . . . . . . . . . . . . . . . . . . . . . . . . . . . . . . .
> *Verse: A:*     *If there's anything that you want* . . . . . . . . . . . . . . . . . . . . . . . . . .
> . . . . . . . . . . . . . . . . . . . . . . . . . . . . . . . . . . . . . .
> . . . . . . . . . . . . . . . . . . . . . . . . . . . . . . . . . . . . . .
> . . . . . . . . . . . . . . . . . . . . . . . . . . . . . . . . . . . . . .

Notice that the first lines of each A section are quite similar, ending with the phrase "everything/anything that you want." In contrast, the lyrics of the bridge section make a more specific statement: "I've got arms that long to hold you." Similarly, the musical qualities of the song change during the bridge section, providing the song with some variation and a transition back to the important final A section. Thus, in AABA form, the bridge usually features a musical lift to the song, both in pitch and harmony. Correspondingly, the lyrics usually suggest some transition in the speaker's way of thinking or a changing course of events in the storyline.

When writing songs in this form, you will find that the first or last line of the verse sections is a good place to put the hook. Some hit AABA songs that use the title/hook in the first line position include Jim Croce's "Time in a Bottle," and Gerry Goffin and Michael Masser's "Do You Know Where You're Going To?," the theme song of the movie *Mahogany.* Marvin Hamlisch's "What I Did for Love," from the hit Broadway musical *A Chorus Line,* features the title in the last two lines of the verse. In the Michael Jackson version of "Ben," the simple title is featured as the first word of each A section or verse as well as the last word of the song. As you can see, the general rule is to feature the hook/title at least once in a strong position, and it's a good bet to weave it into other verses as well.

Remember that the bridge of the song usually serves as an uplifting transitional passage to lead back to the familiar A section, where you might want to repeat the hook again. The typical AABA song has relatively short sections that develop and tie together nicely into one unifed whole. There are variants on the form, like "Cabaret" by John Kander and Fred Ebb, which follows the AABABA pattern (with a coda at the end). The Police even used the basic AABA form in conjunction with a chorus section for "Every Breath You Take," which follows an AABACBA pattern with a coda. But the overall effect of all AABA songs is that of a well-constructed circle that gives the listener a sense of return and completion during the final A section.

### The Verse/Chorus Form

The other basic song form popular today is the verse/chorus form. The typical verse/chorus song features the hook in repetition in the chorus. If you were to examine all the popular song forms today, chances are that you would find this form to be the winner hands down. Some classics that use this pattern include "Paper Roses," "Streets of London," and "Those Were the Days." The familiar Stephen Foster song "Oh Susanna," which James Taylor liked enough to cover on one of his albums, is a great illustration of the pure verse/chorus form:

| | |
|---|---|
| *Verse:* | *Oh, I come from Alabama* |
| | *With my banjo on my knee,* |
| | *And I'm goin' to Lou'siana,* |
| | *My true love for to see;* |
| | *Oh, it rained all night the day I left,* |
| | *The weather it was dry.* |
| | *The sun so hot I froze to death;* |
| | *Susanna, don't you cry.* |
| *Chorus:* | *Oh, Susanna,* |
| | *Don't you cry for me.* |
| | *For I come from Alabama* |
| | *With my banjo on my knee.* |
| *Verse:* | *Late last night,* |
| | *The other day,* |
| | *When everything was still,* |
| | *I thought I saw Susanna* |
| | *Coming down the hill.* |
| | *The buckwheat cake was in her hand* |
| | *A tear was in her eye.* |
| | *I'm goin' to Lou'siana* |
| | *Susanna, don't you cry.* |
| *Chorus:* | *Oh, Susanna,* |
| | *Don't you cry for me.* |
| | *For I come from Alabama* |
| | *With my banjo on my knee.* |

Most popular songs repeat this pattern one or more times, with new lyrics in the verse and the same lyrics in the chorus. Often the music of the verse section is different from that featured in the chorus, but several successful songs have the same basic harmony in both sections, such as "Goodnight, Irene" and "Johnny B. Goode." In most cases, the chorus provides a climactic rhythm and harmonic movement to highlight the important hook section of the song.

Sometimes the chorus of a song consists of something as simple as a phrase with an instrumental section, a vocal arrangement of just a few words or oohs and ahs. Justin Heyward's "Nights in White Satin" creates this kind of impressionistic chorus with great instrumentals. The simple lyric "Yes, I love you/Oh, how I love you" is featured in a long vocal phrase that gives way to a dramatic instrumental section featuring a flute solo. This kind of free-form chorus can be very effective if you have plans for an interesting arrangement to give it a definite form. A strong vocal section with a minimal lyric can create this same effect. Think of the simple lyric in Paul Simon's "The Boxer": "Li-la-li, Li-la-li-la-li-la-li-la-li-la-li." This is an extreme example of the kind of simplicity you should strive for when writing the chorus. Often, however, there is more substance to the lyric, as in the chorus of "Yellow Submarine," where the hook phrase is simply repeated or in the chorus of "Ghostbusters," where the hook is repeated in alternating lines. Although these are also simple choruses, they are strong and effective. They are a good general reminder to make your own chorus a showplace for the all-important hook.

Today's songwriters sometimes prefer variations of the verse/chorus form. The verse/chorus/bridge form (ABC) and forms like ABCBC and ABCABC are just some of the variations that have been used with success. Here, the lyric of the verse, and often that of the bridge, develop the characters, situation, or action in the song, while the words of the chorus provide some simple reflection on the song as a whole. The Beatles' "Ticket to Ride" epitomizes the verse-chorus-bridge form popular today.

|  |  |
|---|---|
| (Verse) A: | *I think I'm going to be sad,* |
|  | . . . . . . . . . . . . . . . . . . . . . . . . . . . . . . . . . . . . |
|  | . . . . . . . . . . . . . . . . . . . . . . . . . . . . . . . . . . . . |
| (Chorus) B: | *She's got a ticket to ride,* |
|  | . . . . . . . . . . . . . . . . . . . . . . . . . . . . . . . . . . . . |
|  | . . . . . . . . . . . . . . . . . . . . . . . . . . . . . . . . . . . . |
|  | . . . . . . . . . . . . . . . . . . . . . . . . . . . . . . . . . . . . |
| (Bridge) C: | *I don't know why she's riding so high,* |
|  | . . . . . . . . . . . . . . . . . . . . . . . . . . . . . . . . . . . . |
|  | . . . . . . . . . . . . . . . . . . . . . . . . . . . . . . . . . . . . |
|  | . . . . . . . . . . . . . . . . . . . . . . . . . . . . . . . . . . . . |

This basic form and its variants give a powerful sense of climax and movement to a song as it mounts through the three sections. There are many variations on this pattern. The Eagles' "Take It to the Limit" and Elton John's "Take Me to the Pilot" follow an AABC pattern. Petula Clark's 1965 hit "Downtown" uses the more extended ABABC. Think of the songs that you know that build dramatically to a big finish. Chances are they have used the verse/chorus/bridge form to give the song its overall feeling of movement.

There are countless variations on the basic forms and there are many successful songwriters who have bent the rules. The best way to choose strong forms for your work is to look at some of the patterns in the songs you like and analyze the parts of their forms. Here's a list of a few songs with forms that you might want to try using as structural models for your own songs.

| | |
|---|---|
| AAA | "We Shall Overcome" as recorded by Pete Seeger (this actually has 10 verses—AAAAAAAAAA) <br> "Colour My World" as recorded by Chicago <br> "Day by Day" from the musical *Godspell* |
| AABA | "Raindrops Keep Fallin' on My Head" as recorded by B.J. Thomas <br> "What I Did for Love" from the Broadway musical *A Chorus Line* <br> "Memories" from the Broadway musical *Cats* <br> "Ben" as recorded by Michael Jackson |
| AAABA | "Baby Grand" as recorded by Billy Joel and Ray Charles |
| Verse/ Chorus | "Those Were the Days" as recorded by Mary Hopkin <br> "Till the End" as recorded by Toto <br> "How Much Love" as recorded by Survivor |
| Chorus/ Verse | "The Most Beautiful Girl" as recorded by Charlie Rich <br> "Diamond Girl" as recorded by Seals and Crofts |
| AABAAB | "Coward of the County" as recorded by Kenny Rogers (it's actually verse/verse/chorus four times, or AABAABAABAAB) <br> "Rock the Night" as recorded by Europe (it's really verse/verse/chorus repeated twice, or AABAAB) |
| AABBCD | "Taxi" as recorded by Harry Chapin |

# 4

# *The Music*

The song is ended
But the melody lingers on.

—*Irving Berlin*

Our friend wrote music
and in that mould he created
gaiety and sweetness and beauty
and twenty-four hours after he had gone
his music filled the air
and in triumphant accents
proclaimed to this world of men
that gaiety and sweetness and beauty
do not die. . . .

—*Oscar Hammerstein II*
(from his poem ''Gershwin'' )

Music is generally defined as consisting of melody, harmony, and rhythm. In songwriting, these elements must not only work together but must also support the lyric. No matter which comes first, the melody or the lyric, they must both follow the same form. As the various elements of a song's music take shape, you will find that each one helps determine aspects of the other. During this process, it is important that the songwriter remain flexible to meet the needs of each element. The overall goal is to create a coherent harmonic and rhythmic texture to frame the all-important melody and lyric of the song.

## Tempo and Feel

There are many different kinds of songs, from cowboy yodels to hardcore punk, but whether you are writing for pop, country, or jazz, you should be able to place your song in one of two basic categories: ballad or uptune. These are designations of tempo or feel and need not have anything to do with the theme of the lyrics. Even though a ballad is the traditional domain of serious themes like love and lament, these themes can also be treated quite effectively in uptunes. Think of "After You've Gone" by Henry Creamer and Turner Layton or "It Never Rains in Southern California" by Albert Hammond and Mike Hazelwood. Rock and roll has given us many uptunes with serious themes. Think of Billy Joel's "Only the Good Die Young" or Creedence Clearwater Revival's "Proud Mary." By the same token, ballads are not always serious or tragic. Many ballads treat uplifting or lighthearted themes. Good examples are "Our House" by Graham Nash and "I'm All Smiles" by Michael Leonard and Herb Martin.

### The Ballad

Originally, the word "ballad" was used to describe a song that told a story in repeated verses. This kind of narrative song required an even, often slow, tempo so that the words could be easily understood. Eventually, ballad came to mean any slow- to medium-tempo song with relatively simple and important lyrics, usually centering on love, longing, or lament. The ballad's rhythmic basis is usually simple and unobtrusive, so a strong melody, wedded to a convincing lyric, is a must.

Many different ballad styles have enjoyed popularity through the years. Some favorite settings include the country waltz, the jazz singer's torch song, and the classic blues lament. Today, the styles of ballads range from simple classics like B.J. Thomas's "Rock and Roll Lullaby" to the rhythmic power ballad common to pop and rock and roll. Dionne Warwick's "I'll Never Love This Way Again" and the Joe Cocker and Jennifer Warnes hit "Up Where We Belong" are good examples of power ballads. The power ballad usually has a driving moderate tempo, with sustained notes and minimal lyrics, a nice middle ground between a true ballad and an uptune. In recent years, the power ballad has enjoyed increasing success on the charts. Try playing a ballad or uptune that you're working on with a power ballad feel. You might find that its easy, yet insistent tempo is an effective compromise.

There are significantly more ballads than uptunes on the charts today. This has been true throughout the history of American popular music. So, no matter which kind of music you write—pop, rock, country, jazz, or blues—the ballad should be a regular in your repertoire.

### The Uptune

An uptune (or up-tempo song) is any song with a medium to fast tempo. As with the ballad, this term refers to the tempo of the song and has nothing to do with its theme. Just because it's an uptune doesn't mean it has to be about a lighthearted subject (although many of them are). The beat and force of the uptune can intensify sad or serious themes quite effectively as in "I Can't Get No Satisfaction," "Mama Told Me (Not to Come)," and "Beat It."

The tempo and force of an uptune may range from the easygoing country beat of Pure Prairie League's "Amie" to the frenzied rhythm and force of Michael Sembello's "Maniac." Though more ballads make it to the top of the charts, the uptune is the backbone of the contemporary sound in all genres and the inspiration for many dance crazes.

## Melody

The melody of a song is the part that is sung. It is not the clever chord progression, the intricate rhythmic structure, or the fantastic guitar solo. This needs to be understood because many songwriters rely on other elements to do the melody's job.

The melody is such an important element of a song that people often refer to a song as a "melody" or a "tune." Even today, when interesting melodies often seem overshadowed by rhythmic and electronic effects, they are still the foundation of good songs. A good melody is a must if you want your song to be a commercial success. It doesn't have to be fancy or complex. The general rule is: keep your song melodies simple and clear-cut.

In all standard song forms, the melody may be broken down into sections, one or more of which is often repeated. Within each section, whether intro, verse, chorus, or bridge, smaller elements of the melody often appear in repeating or imitative patterns. Being able to identify these "subsections" of a melody can help you to analyze songs that you like. This enables you to bring more structure and understanding to your writing.

To explore how small melodic elements are combined into a whole, let's build a melody up from the beginning. This is not the most typical approach to creating a melody—although it is a viable one—but it is the best way to delineate a melody's different parts. The melody that we're building is probably the most common arrangement, but it is still only one of many variations.

The smallest melodic element, aside from a single note, is a *motif* (also called a *motive*). A motif is a small, distinctive grouping of two or more notes. If we compare patterns of melody with those of language, the melodic motif corresponds to a word or short group of words.

Usually a motif must be repeated or at least reused in a recognizably altered form to be considered a true motif. It is rare that you can point to something that only occurs once in a melody and designate it as a motif.

One or more motifs may be developed into a *phrase*. Phrases are commonly two measures long, but they may sometimes be three. Let's take the motif above and extend it into a phrase.

Putting two phrases together gives you a melodic *period*, or *sentence*. (Notice how these terms echo those used to describe language or speech.) The simplest example of this idea is a phrase that repeats.

Often the second phrase serves as an "answer" to a "question" posed by the first.

When you take your four-bar period and either repeat it or create an "answering" period, you have a melodic *paragraph*. The one we have ended with below could be the A section to a standard AABA song.

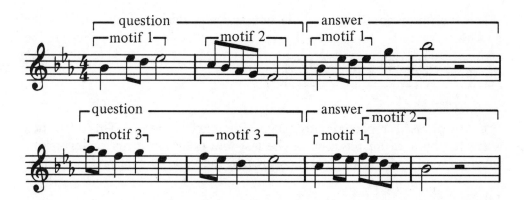

This concept of a melody as component parts can be handy in a number of ways. Although it can be applied to composing, it is often used in the opposite way, for analysis. Breaking down a good melody into its paragraphs, periods, and phrases, and identifying the various motifs and question and answer sections, will help you understand what makes it tick. Conversely, if you have written a melody that just doesn't seem to work as a whole and yet parts of it are so good that you cannot bear to scrap it entirely, an analysis of this type is the best way to begin your doctoring.

### Manipulating Motifs and Phrases

Motifs and phrases may be manipulated in a number of ways. Though these may seem like rather mechanical, uncreative devices, they do generate a lot of usable, melodically related material.

The simplest thing that you can do with a motif or phrase is to repeat it. Thousands of blues, rock, and jazz songs use a repeated riff over changing chords as a starting point. In its most literal cases, this technique creates a forceful tension that arises from the listener's knowing what is coming but having to wait for the performer to get through it. Think of the power that Bruce Springsteen was able to infuse into the song "Pink Cadillac" by repeating a simple four-note motif over twelve bars.

Instead of repeating the motif or phrase exactly, you can transpose it up or down. This is called a *sequence*. Janis Ian's "At Seventeen" uses sequences to preserve the dreamlike quality of the melody without getting monotonous. She starts with a phrase that may be outlined as follows:

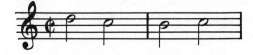

This is then transposed up a whole step and repeated.

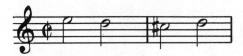

Then the phrase is repeated with a slight difference at the end. This difference is created by a *mirror inversion* of the last few notes. In a mirror inversion, whatever went up in the original goes down by the same interval, and vice versa.

Finally, the phrase is returned to its original pitch but with the same mirror inversion of the last few notes.

A song that is full of sequences is the Beatles' "Ob-la-di, Ob-la-da." As an exercise, go through and identify as many as you can find. Bill Withers's "Lean on Me" makes extensive use of *retrograde inversion* (playing a sequence of notes backwards) throughout, starting at the very beginning of the song.

This song also uses repetition, sequences, and mirror inversion to develop its interesting, varied, yet unified melody. Try singing, playing, or listening to "Lean on Me" and see how many of these you can find and identify.

*Augmentation* and *diminution* are two more ways to alter a melodic unit. *Rhythmic* augmentation or diminution takes the original motif and increases or decreases the time value of each note. An example is in John Denver's "Leaving on a Jet Plane" in which the half-note motif sung to the word "leaving" is echoed in quarter notes on the words "don't know." You can also use *melodic* augmentation or diminution in which you increase or decrease the distance between some of the pitches of a motif. A good example is to be found in the Harold Arlen and E. Y. Harburg classic "Over the Rainbow." The distinctive up-an-octave, down-a-half-step motif comprising the first three notes is repeated twice in the following measures with the octave leap reduced first to a major sixth and then to a minor sixth.

### Vocal Ranges

As a songwriter, you should never lose sight of the fact that your songs must be singable. Unless you are an accomplished singer yourself, you must keep an eye on your melody as it evolves to make sure that it does not exceed the limitations of the average voice. If a song goes too high or too low for a particular singer, it can always be transposed down or up until it is in a suitable key. But if the song is both too high and too low, it is unsingable.

As a general rule, try to limit the range of your melody to an octave. This not only makes it accessible to singers with different vocal ranges without excessive transposing, but also makes it easier for anyone listening to pick up the melody or sing along. Unless you are writing for a virtuoso whose range you know, the absolute limit would be an octave plus a fifth. This is the range of "The Star Spangled Banner" (from the low note on the word "say" in "Oh, say can you see," to the high notes on "red glare" in "And the rockets' red glare" ). With all the complaints about how difficult this song is to sing, you can see how important this aspect of your melody is in determining its singability.

## Harmony

To harmonize a melody is to determine other notes that sound good accompanying it. A melodic line that harmonizes with the melody is called a *countermelody* or *harmony line*. More than two notes sung or played together make up a *chord*. Countermelodies and other elements of arranging are not usually considered part of songwriting, but coming up with a basic harmonization made up of chords is.

### Chords

A chord is named after its *root*. The root of a G Major chord is the note G, for example, and the root of a B-flat Minor Seventh chord is B-flat. The most basic kind of chord is a *triad*, which consists of three notes: the root, the third, and the fifth. The third and the fifth are taken from the scale of the root. Here is the way to build a C Major triad.

You can make this triad a *minor* triad by *flatting* the third (lowering it one half-step).

Taking a minor triad and flatting its fifth gives you a *diminished* triad.

Starting with a major triad and sharping the fifth (raising it one half-step) produces an *augmented* triad.

If you build a triad above each note in a scale, you end up with the most commonly used chords in that key. The Roman numerals naming each chord provide an easy way to refer to these chords in a general manner.

Adding a seventh to each chord gives you what are known as the _diatonic seventh chords_ of a key (diatonic means "of the scale" ).

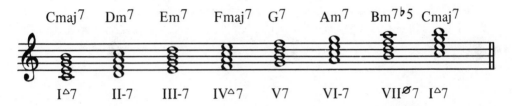

If you play the first four of these diatonic sevenths, you will recognize the opening harmony to the Beatles' "Here, There, and Everywhere."

Major Seventh, Minor Seventh, and Half-Diminished Seventh chords have a distinctly jazzy sound and are often used in blues, rock, or country to add a jazz tinge to a song.

### Cadences and Chord Progressions

Constructing a _chord progression_ entails deciding what chords to use with a melody and when they change. Another name for a chord progression is the _chord changes,_ or simply the _changes,_ to a song.

Of the commonly used chords mentioned above, the most important are the I, IV, and V chords. The I chord is important because it is built on the root of the scale. The I chord gives a feeling of stability and rest, while all of the other chords imply varying degrees of tension. This tension almost always resolves ultimately to the I chord by the song's end. Most melodies end on the first degree (the root) of the scale, too. A chord progression that ends on a chord other than I sounds unfinished or up in the air. Sometimes this is a desirable effect, as in the final ending to "By the Time I Get to Phoenix" by Jim Webb, which ends on a VI Major chord.

A chord or series of chords resolving to the I chord, usually at the end of a phrase or section, make up a formula called a _cadence._ Traditionally, the two main types of final cadence are the V I, or _authentic,_ cadence and the IV I, or _plagal,_ cadence.

There are many common formulas that build on these two cadences.

**IV V I**

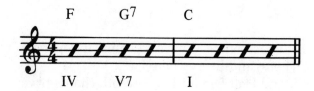

**flat-VII (IV of IV) IV I**

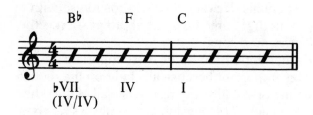

**II V I**

II Major (V of V) V I

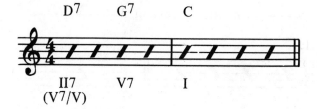

II7    V7    I
(V7/V)

flat-VII (IV of IV) V I

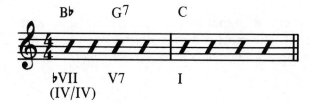

♭VII    V7    I
(IV/IV)

There are other types of cadences that resolve to the V chord (*half* cadences) or to other chords (*deceptive* or *evaded* cadences). The half cadence is often used at the end of a section that repeats before going on; for instance, the first A section of an AABA song.

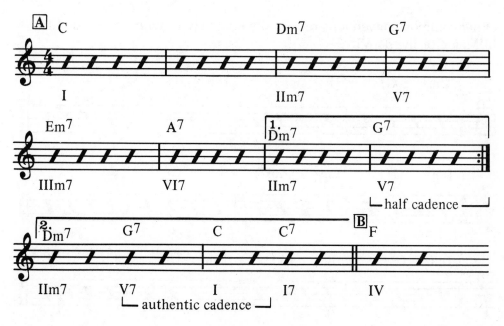

Deceptive cadences are usually used to modulate to a new key.

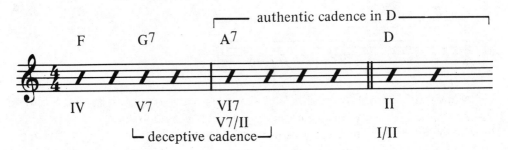

You can also use a deceptive cadence to signal that the song is not over and that a line or two is going to repeat. The most common deceptive cadence for this use is where the I chord is replaced by the VI, its *relative minor.*

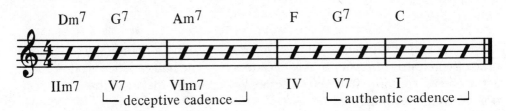

Other common conventions replace the final I chord with the IV, the III, the III Major, or the flat-VI.

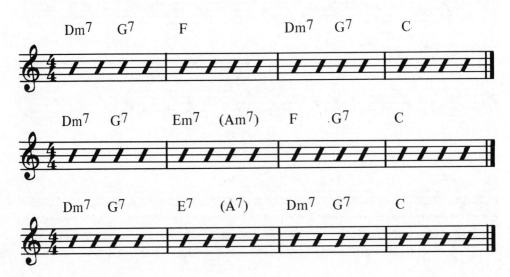

Putting together a logical and workable chord progression takes a bit of knowledge and a lot of practice. If you are an instrumentalist and used to playing chord changes, let your experience guide you when harmonizing your own songs. Although it is not a recommended approach to songwriting, you can learn a lot by writing new melodies to existing chord progressions. In trying to make your new melodies as different as possible from the originals, notice how some chord progressions force you into certain melodic conventions, while others are more open and adaptable.

As you examine different chord progressions, you are bound to find more of these devices, or even entire progressions, that are used over and over again. These are the harmonic conventions of the genre or style you are considering. (You will find some of these pointed out later in the chapters on specific styles.) In harmonizing your songs, be aware that it is extremely difficult to create a truly unique chord progression. It is not even desirable to get too original or far out in your harmonizations; this can cause your song to sound too esoteric or make it too hard for the average musician to learn. There are certainly many successful popular songs that are harmonically complex, but unless you are sure, keep it simple.

## Rhythm

Rhythm is one element that occurs at every moment of the song's duration. There is never a moment during a song when rhythm is not present. Even if there is total silence, it is silence for a certain number of beats. Having a strong sense of rhythm can make the songwriter's job much easier when shaping the melody and harmony of the song. Rhythm is also perhaps the most important unifying force in a song when it comes to blending music with lyrics.

The greatest influence on a song's rhythm is its *meter*. Meter is concerned with the most basic grouping of beats. Most popular songs may be said to be "in two" or "in four." This tells you something about the underlying rhythm since the first beat in each metrical group is stressed, or accented, to some degree.

Many different rhythms can share the same meter. For instance, the Ad Libs' hit "The Boy from New York City" and Madonna's "La Isla Bonita" are both in two (duple meter). "The Boy from New York City" uses the duple meter in a very straightforward manner.

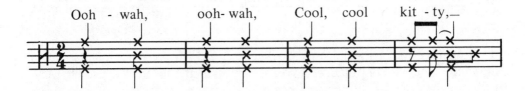

"La Isla Bonita," on the other hand, has a more syncopated (off-the-beat) sophistication to its Caribbean-influenced rhythm.

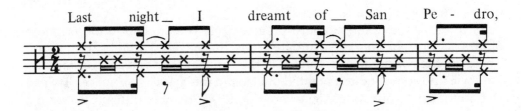

Songs in four (*quadruple* meter) have a secondary accent on the third beat in each metrical group. Traditionally, this secondary accent receives less stress than the accent on one, and this stress is more felt than heard. But in rock and other forms of popular music, the secondary accent becomes the *backbeat*. Although the backbeat is sometimes accented in the traditional, "secondary" manner, often it receives an even heavier accent than the first beat. This is called "turning the beat around." For an example of a subtle, yet noticeable, backbeat, listen to Blondie's "The Tide Is High"; a prominent use of the accented backbeat is in "Will It Go Round in Circles" by Billy Preston.

### Rhythm and Song Style

Sometimes the overall rhythm of a song expresses its particular style or feeling. Song types characterized in large part by rhythm include the waltz (triple meter), bossa nova and samba (syncopated duple meter), funk (highly syncopated duple, quadruple, or *compound duple* [in six] meter), and disco (duple or quadruple meter subdivided into eight or sixteen). In today's world of electronic instruments and computerized effects, rhythm is an important concern for the songwriter. This is especially true if you want to make your song danceable.

## Putting It All Together

As the melody, harmony, and rhythm of a song take shape, there are bound to be adjustments and compromises. Perhaps part of the melody needs to be altered to highlight a particularly pleasing or effective section of the chord progression. Or maybe a chord or two in the harmony sound a little sour or make the melody line difficult to sing. Sometimes altering the tempo of a song is just the thing to bring it into focus. After you have the basic outline for a song's melody, harmony, and rhythm, it should be relatively easy to fine-tune these different elements until they can work together smoothly. If you get stuck while writing one part of a song, you might find it helpful to set it aside for a little while. Many times just getting a fresh look at the problem will bring the solution. Above all, remember that great harmony and rhythm should be unobtrusive and work at all times to support and highlight the melody and lyric of the song.

# 5

# The Song Title

*My favorite thing is titles. I write lots of titles. You can imagine such wonderful things just from the title that you don't always get when you write the song.*

—Richard Thompson

*There's only about five major themes that you could really write about commercially. The trick is to make them sound new. A lot of the times we start from a title; if it's a good title it sums up the whole song. I always feel that a song is really good if you can sum it up in one sentence. Any more than that and you're just spinning your wheels. A lot of times we'll work from a title and get a skeletal sentence here and there and we'll fill in all the spaces. We try to make every sentence support the central theme some way or another.*

—Jim Peterik

## The Importance of a Good Title

Many songwriters feel that a good title is half the song. This may be extreme, but the title is very important, and learning to choose a winner will help you a lot. Whether you're trying to sell your song to a major recording artist, or just trying to get a friend to help you with a demo, the title is the first thing that people know about your song; it is important to make it interesting. Since the title is often repeated in the hook of a song, it also helps people remember the song and enables them to ask for it again!

Many a great song has started out as nothing more than an interesting title, and some songwriters use this "title-first" method regularly to develop songs. Mac Davis was asked by his producer to write a "hook" song, that is, a song with a prominent title and hook. He picked up his guitar, went in the next room, and came up with the title "Baby, Don't Get Hooked on Me" as a joke. As he started to work out the chorus, he realized the potential of the song and finished it on the spot. You know the rest. It's a good idea to use your title in the hook, and to repeat it more than once in the song.

### Title and Hook Placement

Repetition of the title in the hook can be very important to the success of a song, and songwriters favor a number of different patterns. Sometimes the hook is simply repeated throughout the chorus, as in "Take It to the Limit" or "Born in the U.S.A." Other times the hook is repeated in alternating lines of the chorus, as in "Like a Virgin" and "What's Love Got to Do with It." In "Margaritaville" and "Brandy" the hook appears only in the first line of the chorus. "Seasons in the Sun" features the hook in just the second line of the chorus. "Until It's Time for You to Go" has the hook only in the last line. The first or last line of the verse is another key spot for the hook, as in "Happy Together" or "At Seventeen."

A few successful songs do not use conventional hook placement to emphasize the title of the song or don't use a hook at all. "The Rose" mentions the title only in the last line. John Denver's "Annie's Song" doesn't mention its title at all.

### Picking a Good Title

A title should express the message of the song in a nutshell. The title is usually repeated in the first or last line of the song's verse or chorus—the hook. All the other lyrics serve as a framework for this important line.

Most modern song titles have a conversational tone, as in "Let's Hear It for the Boy" or "What's Love Got to Do with It." A few hit titles use phrasing that is not found in day-to-day conversation. This can make a title sound important and fresh, as in "The First Time Ever I Saw Your Face" and "Killing Me Softly with His Song." Notice how the formal tone of the language in these titles intensifies the beauty and sincerity of the speaker's message. Don't let this kind of a title be too flowery though. Remember, song lyrics are not poetry and the majority of successful songs stick with conversational language to reach out to the average listener.

### How Long Should a Title Be?

As a rule, a title should have few words. Many successful songs have one-word titles. Just a few are "Swanee," "Imagination," "People," "Reunited," "Fame," and "Maniac", not to mention the endless stream of one-word name titles—"Jean," "Rosalie," "Elvira." Titles of two or more words should form a meaningful phrase; the more concise, the better. A quick glance at the Top 100 charts will show very few titles of more than five words. Exceptions to this rule are "If Loving You Is

Wrong (I Don't Want to Be Right)," "Don't It Make My Brown Eyes Blue," and "Tie a Yellow Ribbon 'Round the Ole Oak Tree." A few great titles are quite long. This usually creates a comic effect as in "I've Got Tears in My Ears from Lying on My Back and Crying over You."

Try to create a title that is concise and catchy and conveys the essence of the song. A song title can never be too simple. Keep in mind that the title you choose will probably be repeated in the lyric of the song's hook, so try for titles that have a natural and effective rhythm and sound.

### The Speaker's Voice

It is important to consider the voice of the speaker in the title as well as in the lyric. If the speaker is simply the narrator of the song's story, as in "Delta Dawn" or "Eleanor Rigby," you probably don't want to include the speaker in the title. Often the speaker is a participating character in the events of the song. This may be apparent in the song's title, as in Wham's "Wake Me up Before You Go-Go" or "Every Breath You Take" by the Police. Although as a general rule you want to limit yourself to one speaker per song, some duets and novelty songs incorporate two or more speakers. "Frankie and Johnnie" is a classic example of a song with two speakers; actually, there are three including the narrator. Cat Stevens's "Father and Son" uses the voice of both characters mentioned in the title in dialogue. If you want to suggest the presence of more than one speaker in a song title, make sure to be clear in the lyrics which character is speaking at a given time. Feature the different voices in different sections of the song, with their own characteristic harmony, rhythm, and range. For further discussion of the role of the speaker in lyrics, see the section on character in Chapter 6 (page 58 to 77).

### Statements and Declarations

Using simple statements in titles is a good way to keep the message of the song clear. Although a title need not be a complete phrase, it is often effective to use a simple sentence to express the main theme of a song. Think of Stevie Wonder's "You Are the Sunshine of My Life," Billy Joel's "It's Still Rock and Roll to Me," and Queen's "Another One Bites the Dust." Sometimes the statement is completed in a parenthetical phrase, as in Tony Orlando and Dawn's "He Don't Love You (Like I Love You)" or The Eurythmics' "Sweet Dreams (Are Made of This)." More rarely, two complete statements are expressed in a title, again with the help of parentheses. There's Daryl Hall and John Oates's "I Can't Go for That (No Can Do)" and George Harrison's "Give Me Love (Give Me Peace on Earth)." Titles that form complete statements or declarations should be reinforced in the hook of your song. The statement you choose should sum up the theme of the song in a nutshell.

### Questions

Many songwriters have used questions to create provocative titles. Questions are especially effective title choices because they interest the listener in learning their answer: "Where Did Our Love Go," "Why Can't We Be Friends?," "Will It Go Round in Circles". Questions that suggest an answer and therefore require no answer are called rhetorical questions. These make extremely effective titles. Tina Turner's question, "What's Love Got to Do with It" suggests the answer: Not a whole lot. Rhetorical questions are more often directed to the general listener as in "How Can You Mend a Broken Heart" (not too easily). "Is That All There Is"—the speaker's disappointment seems insurmountable and the answer is yes. Notice that many titles that use questions do not incorporate the question mark. Although this is not grammatical, it has become today's standard in the music industry.

### Requests and Commands

A suggestion or request has always been a good framework for a title, as in "Please Come to Boston" or "Let's Go Crazy." But a surprising number of titles in recent years have a commanding tone: "Beat It," "Drive," "Wake Me up Before You Go-Go." This kind of title is forceful and provocative because it suggests great urgency and boldness on the part of the speaker. This type of title is representative of the spirit and mood of the 1980s and of the personality of today's performer. A request or command in a title suggests that the speaker is addressing one person in a particular situation. But there are a few that are directed to the world at large, and these can be very powerful: "Get up and Boogie," "Listen to What the Man Said," "Take It Easy."

## Sources for Titles

There are many approaches to writing a title and many different sources of good title material. Here are the basic types of titles favored by professional songwriters and some tips on how to choose your own titles.

### Universal Sentiments

Many song titles express an idea or a feeling that is understood by everyone. It might be a universal truth: "Love Hurts," "There's No Place like Home for the

Holidays," "You Can't Always Get What You Want." A title may express a common feeling, something that everyone has experienced or thought at one time or another. Think of "Wishing You Were Here," "(I Can't Get No) Satisfaction," "Help Me Make It Through the Night." The ideas and feelings expressed in these titles can be understood and appreciated by most people, so it's no wonder that lyricists and songwriters consistently favor this type of song title.

When choosing titles like these, try to stick to themes that express ideas and feelings that are very familiar to you. Don't try to write a song like "You're Having My Baby" unless you have a gut-level understanding of what it is like to be an expectant father. Many important moments in your life and in the lives of others can provide good title material. Staying with subjects you know and care about is the best guard against titles that are confusing or clichéd.

### Current Events and Social Trends

Some songwriters have used world events and the mood of the times as a source of title material. Usually these are songs of protest or social unity. Keep in mind that current issues grow stale in time unless they are treated as a symbol of a larger social problem or trend. The economic problems of the Depression years brought such classics as "Brother, Can You Spare a Dime," "Empty Pocket Blues," and "My Forgotten Man." The World Wars spawned patriotic titles like "Praise the Lord and Pass the Ammunition" and "Over There." By contrast, the Vietnam War inspired many songs of protest like "Waist Deep in the Big Muddy," "Your Flag Decal Won't Get You into Heaven Anymore," and "Draft Dodger Rag." The escalation of the nuclear arms race and the prospect of a world holocaust has inspired such titles as "Last Night I Had the Strangest Dream," "Whose Garden Was This?," and "Who's Next?"

The civil rights and black power movements prompted such titles as "We Shall Overcome," "Society's Child," and "We Are Family." The women's rights movement inspired "I Will Survive" and "I Am Woman." The first woman in space was honored in the title of Al Green's "Ride, Sally Ride." The gay right movement prompted "I Am What I Am." The erosion of the family unit has caused such titles as "D-I-V-O-R-C-E" and "Husbands and Wives." Unemployment and the sagging economy stimulated "A Working Man Can't Get Nowhere Today."

As you gather ideas for titles from current affairs, be sure you choose an issue or event that is of lasting import or that stands as a symbol for a larger social concern. Although the song "Ohio" is about one particular event, the Kent State shooting, it is a moment in history that will symbolize domestic unrest and its tragic results for years to come.

## Characters and People

Hundreds of tunes use fictional characters or real people in their titles. These songs usually paint a portrait of the person, either to depict a slice of life—"Leader of the Pack," "Please, Mr. Postman," "Mr. Bojangles," "Hard Headed Woman"—or to create a character who represents a larger aspect of the human condition—"Mr. Wonderful," "Bad, Bad Leroy Brown," "Superfly," and "Twentieth Century Fox." Public figures, past and present, make good subjects for song titles, such as "Lady Godiva;" "Bette Davis Eyes;" "Vincent," a portrait of Vincent Van Gogh; "Sir Duke," Stevie Wonder's tribute to Ellington; or Merle Haggard's "Leonard," about his friend and songwriting buddy Tommy Collins. Fictitious characters have often proved to be fascinating subjects for song titles. Think of "Mack the Knife," "Me and Mrs. Jones," "Purple People Eater," and "Eleanor Rigby." Fictional characters from literature and film have also been recalled in song titles. "Dorothy," by Hugh Prestwood, muses on why Dorothy didn't stay in the Land of Oz. "Richard Cory" was borrowed by Paul Simon from the character of the poem by Edward Arlington Robinson. Even animal characters have made their appearances in titles of popular songs. There's the pony "Wildfire," "Ben," a love song to a rat, and oh, yes, "Muskrat Love." If you use a real person for the subject of your title, choose someone whom people are familiar with or can relate to on a personal level. If you use a fictitious character from literature or film for your title, there should be enough interesting material about him or her to develop a whole song. If you are introducing your own fictional character in a title, choose an intriguing name and be sure you can tell his or her story in the space of the song.

## Places

Names of places have served as titles for quite a few hits, including "Oklahoma!," "MacArthur Park," "Kansas City." Place names also work nicely in a phrase: "Do You Know the Way to San Jose?," "Moonlight in Vermont," "Born in the U.S.A."

Not only does a place name provide an interesting setting for the action of the song, it can also invoke a certain time period and even a certain type of music. Places in the American South and West, and south of the border, help to create a country feel as in "The Tennessee Waltz," "El Paso," "I Believe the South Is Gonna Rise Again." Urban settings tend to be more appropriate for rock and roll, rhythm and blues, and pop titles, as in "Please Come to Boston," "Living for the City," "The Night Chicago Died," "Up on the Roof." The New Orleans and Delta area suggests a blues or early ragtime jazz feeling—"Basin Street Blues," "Mississippi Mud," and "Way Down Yonder in New Orleans." Harlem brings to mind the golden age of jazz—"Take the A-Train" and "Harlem Nocturne." Foreign and exotic places usually also create a tone of romance or adventure and often invoke the area's own native musical styles, as in "The Girl from Ipanema," "Caribbean Queen (No More Love on the Run)," and "Lisbon Antigua."

Certain places bring to mind important world situations or events. "Bangladesh" was written as an appeal for the victims of a devastating famine. Specific places may also serve to represent larger geographic or demographic areas. For example, Billy Joel's "Allentown" used Allentown, Pennsylvania, to reflect the average lower–middle–class American town. The titles "Harper Valley PTA" and "Pleasant Valley Sunday" evoke visions of suburban and middle-American life-styles.

General place names give a title a more universal feeling, such as "On the Street Where You Live," "Up a Lazy River," and "Under the Boardwalk." Metaphorical and fictitious places have made some very imaginative titles—"Heartbreak Hotel," "Stairway to Heaven," "An Octopus's Garden."

If you use a place name in your title, try to pick a place that agrees with details in the lyrics or is a natural match for the musical style of the song. Stay away from using places that you really are not familiar with or cannot imagine in detail.

### Objects

Many songwriters have used objects in song titles when they want to create a personal tone—"Diamond Ring," "Three Coins in a Fountain," "Paper Roses." Mentioning the body, or parts of it, intensify this effect, as in "These Eyes," "Goin' Out of My Head," "How Can You Mend a Broken Heart?" Imaginary or metaphorical objects have made many a great title—"Love Potion Number Nine," "Peace Train," "Purple Rain," and "Chariots of Fire" are just a few.

Try to choose objects that will help suggest a situation or say something about the characters in the song. If your title includes an imaginary object, be sure that the object's essence can be communicated in the space of the song.

### Conditions and States of Mind

Titles that convey conditions and states of mind provide a good framework for a personal message or mood. Think of "Busted," "Bewitched, Bothered, and Bewildered," and "Upside Down." These descriptive titles usually suggest one person's view of himself or herself or of the world at large. This type of title may also take the form of a descriptive phrase: "Blinded by the Light," "All Shook Up," "Hopelessly Devoted to You."

### Actions and Activities

Verbs are very effective as titles because of their strong suggestion of movement and visual imagery. Songs like "Dancin' in the Streets" and "Groovin' " invite the listener to participate, at least vicariously, in some exciting activity.

## Dates and Times

Times of day can be used to give a feeling of immediacy and excitement, as in Gary "U.S." Bonds's version of "Quarter to Three" or the Gladys Knight and the Pips rendition of "Midnight Train to Georgia." Titles that use times of day can also suggest daily routine—"9 to 5," "Morning Train (Nine to Five)," and "Sunday Morning Coming Down."

Days of the week in titles often give the listener a feeling of familiarity and involvement—"Monday, Monday," "Pleasant Valley Sunday," "Saturday Night's Alright for Fighting." Months can create a more wistful tone—"September Song," "April Showers," "December 1963 (Oh What a Night)." Using a present or near-present time frame in a title can create an urgent or personal tone, especially where romance is concerned—"This Magic Moment," "It's Now or Never," "Ten Minutes Ago." A little more reflective are titles that deal with the speaker's immediate past or future—"Will You Still Love Me Tomorrow?," "Touch Me in the Morning," "What a Difference a Day Makes." Remember that periods of time can be metaphors for the larger past or future, as in the titles "Yesterday," "Tomorrow," and "Sunrise, Sunset." These serve to create a deeper or more universal sense of reminiscence, hope, or longing. There is even room for obviously fanciful time, as in "Eight Days a Week" or "The Twelfth of Never."

Specific moments in the speaker's larger past and future can suggest long-standing relationships and sentiments as in "The First Time Ever I Saw Your Face," "The Last Time I Saw Paris," "That'll Be the Day." Titles that include the ages of characters in the song can give a personal touch—"When I'm Sixty-four," "You Are Sixteen," "At Seventeen." More general time periods, or ongoing moments in the speaker's life, have a more universal appeal—"Those Were the Days," "Rainy Days and Mondays," "One Fine Day."

Specific moments in history (real or fictionalized) usually deal with topics of universal importance: "The Night Chicago Died" and "The Night They Drove Old Dixie Down." Large historical time frames like those suggested in "The Great Mandala," "The Circle Game," and "In the Year 2525" offer a powerful look at the past and future of the human race.

"Forever," "never," "always," and "from now on" are used in titles to express infinite time and the unchanging quality of human love or longing: "From This Moment On," "Always Wanting You (But Never Touching You)," "Never Can Say Goodbye." The subject of time itself makes strong title material as in "Time in a Bottle" and "It's Going to Take Some Time."

## Metaphor and Simile

Metaphors can be powerful symbols in song titles—"Love Is a Battlefield" and "We Are the World." Similes can be just as effective: "Like a Rolling Stone," "Feels

Like the First Time," "Like a Virgin." Sometimes the metaphor or simile in a song title becomes apparent when we hear the lyric. The words of "Red Rubber Ball" reveal that the title is an evocative simile for the setting sun. Or think of the Moody Blues revealing that their "Nights in White Satin" are "letters I've written." Choose metaphors and similes that are strong and fresh and yet are either immediately understandable to the listener or fully elaborated in the song lyrics.

Metaphors may be used to link unlikely words to form unusual and meaningful images or ideas. These can be quite clever. "Love Hangover," "Earth Angel," and "Killing Me Softly with His Song" are just a few imaginative titles that use metaphor in this way.

### Puns and Wordplay

Puns can be fun in a title and contribute to its catchiness, as in "She's Acting Single, I'm Drinking Double," "All My Exes Live in Texas," and "Ain't It Amazin' Gracie." Usually puns give a humorous tone to a title, although sometimes they provide an ironic twist as in "Private Eyes."

### Numbers

Numbers can be very catchy in titles and are used surprisingly often, as in "Revolution Number Nine," "Three Times a Lady," "50 Ways to Leave Your Lover," and "96 Tears." The numbers one and two are often used in titles to portray human relationships, or the lack thereof—"One Is the Loneliest Number," "Still the One," "Just the Two of Us," and "Torn Between Two Lovers."

### Repetitions

Repeated words can make for a noticeable and insistent title—"Bad, Bad Leroy Brown," "Fly, Robin, Fly." It's not surprising that many hits use repetition in their titles; repetition helps convey the intensity and excitement that makes people remember the song. Don't hesitate to repeat words in your titles, but be careful not to overdo it. A triple repetition is quite strong—"Say Say Say," "I Want You, I Need You, I Love You." Four repeated words is the absolute limit: "(Shake, Shake, Shake) Shake Your Booty." Try to choose words that are naturally repeated in conversation, as in "Round and Round," "No More Tears (Enough Is Enough)," and "Time After Time." Repetition can make a title very clever when the repeated words have different shades of meaning, as in "Please, Please Me," "He Don't Love You (Like I Love You)," and "I Want to Be Wanted." If you use repetition, you are automatically using rhyme as well, and this adds to the catchiness of the title's sound. Keep an ear out for words that are naturally repeated in conversations and you've got some great title material.

*Rhyme*

Using rhyming words in a title has proved an effective way to frame a hit: "(We're Gonna) Rock Around the Clock," "My Guy," "The Name Game," and "Blue Bayou."

*Repeated Sounds*

The repetition of a consonant sound, as in "Seasons in the Sun," and "Roses Are Red (My Love)," is called *alliteration,* while repeating a vowel sound, as in "Reason to Believe," "Sweet Dreams," is known as *assonance.* These two devices are a sure way to make a title pleasing to the ear and memorable. Using obvious alliterations, for example on accented syllables, reinforces the title's rhythm and adds punch, as in "The Way We Were," "My Boyfriend's Back," and "Philadelphia Freedom." Subtler repetitions are also quite effective—"Once in Awhile," "Touch Me in the Morning," "Torn Between Two Lovers."

Songwriters favor the repetition of vowel sounds to add sparkle to a title, although the effect is not as obvious as that of alliteration. Think of "Hey! Baby," "Owner of a Lonely Heart," "Ruby Tuesday." You will be surprised at how many titles use this technique. Using both assonance and alliteration can be doubly catchy. Examples include "The Coward of the County," "You Light Up My Life," and "Karma Chameleon." Adding word repetitions intensifies this effect: "Lay, Lady, Lay," "(Hey, Won't You Play) Another Somebody Done Somebody Wrong Song."

*Familiar Phrases*

Familiar phrases make for memorable titles. Just a few are "Beginner's Luck," "Come What May," "Que Será, Será," "Under My Thumb," and "Knock on Wood." A good techinique is to give a familiar phrase an ironic twist like "Hurts So Good," "Let's Face the Music and Dance," and "Total Eclipse of the Heart."

Titles of much older songs are sometimes reused. The Christmas carol title "Joy to the World" was borrowed by Three Dog Night for their hit song about Jeremiah the bullfrog. Bruce Springsteen reused the title from an old Arthur Schwartz showtune for his own hit "Dancing in the Dark." Since song titles are not protected by international copyright laws, they can be used again, but usually years later and with an entirely new slant.

Make a note of the familiar phrases you hear and read each day that might make interesting song titles. These can be powerful because they are already familiar to people who long ago decided these phrases were catchy. Here are some examples that might make good title material. Notice how each one suggests an interesting situation or story line.

"The Lights Are On but Nobody's Home"
"Catch You Later"
"Between a Rock and a Hard Place"
"He Won't Let Up"
"Just Say No"
"Take Me to Your Leader"

### Pop Culture

Current fads and catch-phrases have always been title material for songwriters, but keep in mind the public interest is usually short-lived. Unless you have a way of getting your song released and distributed at the height of a fad's popularity, you'll be stuck with a song in need of a major rewrite. Fads and catch-phrases have successfully spawned such songs as "Doin' the Raccoon," "Convoy," "Where's the Beef?," and "PacMan Fever." The thing to remember about this type of title is that there is usually only one successful song per fad, and its success depends on a timely release.

### About Music

Many successful titles refer to their own musical styles. This is particularly true of blues, country, and rock songs: "You'd Rather Have Blues," "Play that Funky Music," "Drinking a Beer and Singing a Country Song." Some songs even refer to songwriting or to the song itself: "I Write the Songs," "Sad Songs (Say So Much)," "This One's for You." Other song titles refer to the band: "We're an American Band," "Sgt. Pepper's Lonely Hearts Club Band," "Band on the Run." A title may depict a musician or singer, like "Piano Man," "Mr. Tambourine Man," "Guitar Man." If a song has a particularly strong rhythm, you might want to point it out, as in "Hit Me With Your Rhythm Stick" and "Love Beat." If the feel or the groove of your song is particularly important, frame a title to suit that: "She Bop," "Funkytown," "Groovin'," "Good Vibrations." Using a musical reference can be an effective way of drawing attention to the performer and to the music and the message of the song. Just make sure that the style of music or musician or band you refer to is in keeping with the style of the song itself.

### Generic Lyric Syllables and Nonsense Words

Many pop and rock songs contain generic lyrics syllables in their title like "La La La La La La" and "Na Na Hey Hey Kiss Him Goodbye." Related nonsense words can serve a title in the same way, as in "Boogie Oogie Oogie," "Zip-A-Dee-Do-Dah," and "She Bop." This technique was particularly popular among songwriters of the 1950s—"Da Doo Ron Ron," "Do Wah Diddy Diddy," "Shimmy, Shimmy, Ko-Ko-Bop." These titles usually appear prominently in the refrain of the song and can make for a very catchy and upbeat hook. Titles that contain generic syllables invite the listener to dance or sing along with the song—or at least to remember its novel lyric.

### Popular Dance

Dance crazes have produced a lot of hit songs. Just think of "The Varsity Drag," "The Jerk," "The Monkey," "Do the Freddie," "Do the Hustle." The twist was perhaps the all-time winner as title material—"Do the Twist," "The Peppermint Twist," "Let's Twist Again Like We Did Last Summer." Spoofs on dance titles have been novelty successes as well: "The Monster Mash," "The Mouse," "The Nurse." Although the title is key to the success of a dance song, the crucial element is the dance itself, which depends on good dance steps. Many songs with dance themes actually inspired dance crazes, but be aware of current trends in popular dance before attempting to direct them.

### Suggestive Titles

Suggestive titles are very popular today. In fact, they are no longer merely suggestive, they come right out and say it. Madonna's "Like a Virgin" and George Michael's "I Want Your Sex" are just two of the suggestive themes that the mainstream songwriter had to dress up in previous years. Hitherto untalked about themes, from pre- and extramarital sex to gay love, are freely addressed in today's hits. These sexy titles work well for the artists who can pull them off, though you don't want to go overboard with them, or you might limit your song's performability to only the young and outspoken.

# 6

# *The Lyric*

*The most important ingredient of a good song is sincerity. Let the song be yours and yours alone. However important, however trivial, believe it. Mean it from the bottom of your heart, and say what is on your mind as carefully, as clearly, as beautifully as you can.*

*—Oscar Hammerstein II*

The words to a song are called the lyric (sometimes lyrics). Song lyrics resemble poetry in many ways, for both use rhythm, rhyme, and sound to communicate ideas and emotions. But there is one important difference: a poem is designed to stand alone, while lyrics are created to work with the musical elements of a song—melody, harmony, and rhythm—to create a meaningful whole. Many of the best song lyrics seem vague and flat when read or spoken aloud as "poems." They come alive only when sung.

Because good song lyrics must work with the music of a song to communicate ideas to the listener, the lyric must fit naturally with the rhythm of the melody, and with the general tone and feel of the music. The musical highpoints of the song should feature lyrics central to the song's main theme, especially during the hook, or at the beginning and end of song sections. The music must work to provide a good frame for the message of the lyric. At the same time, good lyrics must stand aside for instrumental sections and turnarounds and tell the story in light of the mood and message of the music.

## Developing the Theme by Answering the Important Questions

You may know the old formula for writing a good newspaper article: answer the questions who?, what?, when?, where?, how?, and why? While you don't want your song lyrics to sound like newspaper articles, the inclusion of some of these basic facts is integral to the development of a song's theme. Song lyrics use metaphor, allusion, tone, and imagery to create interesting nuances in the message, guiding the listener to "read between the lines." These artistic elements are what give the lyric "personality" and add depth to its purely factual meaning.

Usually a song answers two or three of these important questions and it may even ignore other questions to add a mysterious or fragmented quality to the song's overall storyline. Since emotional and spiritual issues are often a part of a popular song's message, it is not concerned with factual answers. But even the simplest or most esoteric lyrics develop the theme by providing the listener with factual information, though this may be couched in symbolism and featured in repetition.

### What, Why, and How: The Theme and the Message

Many songs that answer the what and the how of their theme leave the question of why to be answered by the listener or perhaps suggest that this question is unanswerable. Stevie Wonder's and Paul McCartney's "Ebony and Ivory" focuses on the hope of racial brotherhood, as symbolized by the easy mutuality of the black and white keys of the piano. In the classic "The Lady Is a Tramp," the main character is developed largely by answering the question of why she is known as such. She "gets too hungry for dinner at eight" and she "loves the theater, but never comes late." Because of these and other violations of the upper-class, urbane life-style, the singer explains, "That's why the lady is a tramp."

Songs that deal primarily with the what, how, and why of things express some philosophical idea that usually does not require a detailed portrait of character or situation. The Electric Light Orchestra's "All Over the World" and Tom Clay's version of "What the World Needs Now Is Love" focus on the what, how, and why of brotherly love. Sometimes this kind of theme can be more personal as in Tina Turner's song hit, "What's Love Got to Do with It". The classic "These Foolish Things," by Eric Maschwitz and Jack Strachey, which focuses mainly on the what and why of the theme, and uses a simple listing technique to make its point. Objects like a "cigarette that bears a lipstick's traces" and an "airline ticket to romantic places" answer the question of what "foolish things remind me of you." The character of the love the speaker has lost is subtly illustrated through the many things and shared experiences that he remembers from their time together.

When writing lyrics that answer the what, why, and how, it is important that the speaker or narrator express a personal view of the theme. Otherwise, the philosophical message can seem preachy or insincere. If your theme focuses on the what, why, and how of a personal experience, be sure to illustrate the specific effects and results that cause the speaker to feel the way he or she does.

### Who? The Speaker and the Characters

All lyrics have at least one character and that is the speaker of the song as portrayed by the vocalist. This character may be simply a narrator who relates the story or message of the song, as in the Beatles' recording of "She's Leaving Home" or Jim Croce's "Bad, Bad Leroy Brown." These songs often portray another character in detail, and the speaker is never identified by the words "I," "me," or "we." It is always "she" or "he" to illustrate the story of a runaway girl, or bad Mr. Brown, respectively. But no matter how detached from the action of the song, a narrator is still a character. Think about the narrator's standpoint with regard to the main events in the lyric. In "She's Leaving Home" we come to know something about the narrator, who has a superhuman knowledge of the details of the story and is moved by events enough to say "bye-bye" as she goes.

Many times the speaker is not just a narrator but a participating character in the action of the story. Here the words "I" and "me" are used to identify the speaker. The most common relationship described in song lyrics involves two characters in love, about to be in love, or dealing with a love that has somehow ended. Thus the word "you" often indicates the presence of the loved one, as in Stevie Wonder's "I Just Called to Say I Love You" and Gordon Lightfoot's "If You Could Read My Mind." Another way to create this relationship is with the words "us" and "we," as in the song hit "Up Where We Belong" by Joe Cocker and Jennifer Warnes. The other characters in a song can be more specifically named, as in Deniece Williams's "Let's Hear It for the Boy" and Michael Jackson's "Billie Jean."

There are other types of relationships treated by song lyrics. One common technique is the general address, where the speaker is talking to the listener. Here the word "you" is used to refer to the listening audience. In Dolly Parton's "9 to 5" the speaker represents one employee addressing others. Air Supply's "The One That You Love" offers advice to the common man.

If you use abstract characters in your own song lyrics, be sure that we get to know them well during the course of the song. Don't try to introduce too many characters in one song unless you're sure that they serve an important purpose. In Paul Simon's "50 Ways to Leave Your Lover," several characters are mentioned, but they are each a generic representative of the dissatisfied lover. "Maxwell's Silver Hammer" also features several characters, but each is described in a detailed cameo. In general, you should stick to two or three characters, including the speaker, per song. Remember, you only have a short period of time to introduce them and make them memorable and interesting.

### Where? The Situation or Environment

Song lyrics should build a strong situation or environment. If the actual place or setting is not important, the emotional whereabouts of the characters should be developed instead. Sometimes the physical setting of a song provides its theme, as in Madonna's "La Isla Bonita," where the speaker's dream of San Pedro provides the imagery for a romantic dream. Or it could be a more general setting as in Eddie Rabbitt's "I Love a Rainy Night." Whatever setting you choose, be sure to give details that bring it alive for the listener. Merle Haggard's country hit "Swinging Doors" portrays a man who considers a barroom his "new home." The lyric takes care to create the surroundings with details like the "smoke-filled bar" with "swinging doors, a jukebox, and a bar stool," and "a flashing neon sign." With these details the writer has indeed created an atmosphere "just right for heartache."

If your song lyric uses a physical setting to develop the song's theme, you might want to make a list of the elements of the landscape that best evoke its essence. Recognizable images are most effective and will help you to avoid getting bogged down with too much detail. Even a simple lyric like Stevie Wonder's "I Just Called to Say I Love You" suggests a setting in which the speaker must be near a phone. David Bowie's "Let's Dance" probably takes place on a dance floor, while Madonna's "Like a Virgin" probably refers to a bedroom. Even if your setting is not readily apparent, take the time to think through the environment of the song, and see if you can't add some details that might make the lyric more alive by placing it in a meaningful surrounding.

### When? The Time Frame

All lyrics suggest a time frame, and the lyricist should be able to pinpoint the time period when the song takes place. Most often the song is in the present tense as indicated by the verbs "am," "is," and "are." Robbie Nevil's "Wot's It to Ya" and "Baby, Come to Me" by Patti Austin and James Ingram feature a direct address by the speaker in the present tense. The present tense is a natural choice if you want to communicate a sense of immediacy and action.

The future tense can also be quite effective, as in "Every Breath You Take" by the Police. Here, although the speaker conveys his message in the present tense, it makes a statement about the future: "I'll be watching you." The Eagles' "Heartache Tonight" effectively addresses the more immediate future. In "When Doves Cry" by Prince, the time period is dependent on a specific activity. Reflection

on the past is also effective, especially if you want to induce feelings of sentiment or regret. "The Way We Were" and "Yesterday" are moving portraits of the
speakers' pasts. Sometimes the time frame of a lyric includes a combination of
past, present, and future. Helen Reddy's hit recording "Delta Dawn" describes
the fallen figure of a woman in the present: "She's forty-one and her mama still
calls her 'Baby'. " But in a later verse her unhappy story is described in the past
tense: "In her younger days, they called her Delta Dawn." The time frame of these
lyrics spans about two decades, and by taking the time to describe the events
of Delta's youth, intensifies the pathetic quality of her life story.

Whatever time frame you choose for your song, be sure to stick with it
throughout. Don't switch tenses unless you are intentionally providing the listener
with a coherent picture of another time. If your lyric centers on the past or future,
keep in mind that they are still being delivered by the speaker in the present
tense. Although some lyrics identify the particular time of an occurrence, as
in the opening line of "Sgt. Pepper's Lonely Hearts Club Band" or "She's Leaving
Home," don't feel obligated to tell the listener the exact time the events happen.

## The Lyric Form

The ability to create unified and logical song forms is an essential skill for any
songwriter. In fact, a good marriage of words and music cannot occur until the
underlying structure of a song has been outlined. The sections that follow provide an overview of the basic song forms popular today, and some general rules
about the structure of lyric imposed by these forms and their variants.

### The AABA Form

Sometimes you'll see the AABA (verse/verse/bridge/verse) pattern in a song.
These songs contain no chorus but usually feature a transitional bridge section
in its place and the hook/title phrase is featured strongly in the verse sections,
as in the Streisand hit "The Way We Were."

Songwriters use this structure to evoke the sound of the traditional AABA form
used in many of the songs of the twenties, thirties, and forties, like "Blue Skies"
and "The Man I Love." Because of its heritage in the pop, jazz, and show music
of yesteryear, the AABA form gives a song a romantic or nostalgic quality. For
this reason, songwriters use the form mainly for ballads. This is particularly effective when the theme of the lyric centers around reminiscence, loss, or tradi-
tionalism. Michael Jackson's "Ben" uses AABA form to evoke the sincerity and
innocence of a child's devotion to his unconventional pet. "Everything Old Is

New Again" uses the AABA structure in an easy-going uptune with a nostalgic theme.

## The Verse/Chorus Form

Many of today's song lyrics follow a simple verse/chorus pattern. This form is simple and powerful and is much used in country music, rock, pop, and blues. In this form, the title is usually featured prominently in the chorus section of the song as in "Take It to the Limit" or "9 to 5." The lyrics of the verses contain the details and plot development, while the chorus repeats some reflection of the main theme of the song. In the first verse of Carly Simon's "You're So Vain," we get a detailed picture of a vain character in his high-style surroundings, right down to his hat "strategically dipped below one eye" and his apricot scarf. The chorus, "You're so vain, you probably think this song is about you," provides a simple ironic commentary. In the second verse of the song, we get more details about the character, then the chorus repeats.

## Variations on the Verse/Chorus Form

Songwriters sometimes prefer the verse/chorus/bridge form (ABC) and variations like ABCBC. Here, the lyrics of the verses, and often those of the bridge, develop the characters, situation, or action, while the words of the chorus provide some simple reflection or commentary on the song as a whole. The Beatles' "Ticket to Ride" uses the verse/chorus/verse/bridge pattern to give the song an overall sense of variety and movement.

> (Verse) A:    *I think I'm going to be sad,* ...........................
>
> (Chorus) B:     *She's got a ticket to ride,* ...........................
>
> (Verse) A:    *She said that living with me* ..........................
>
> (Chorus) B:     *She's got a ticket to ride,* ...........................
>
> (Bridge) C:      *I don't know why she's riding so high,* ...............

A: (Verse)        *She said that living with me* . . . . . . . . . . . . . . . . . . . . . . . . . . . . .
                  . . . . . . . . . . . . . . . . . . . . . . . . . . . . . . . . . . . . . . . . . . .
                  . . . . . . . . . . . . . . . . . . . . . . . . . . . . . . . . . . . . . . . . . . .
                  . . . . . . . . . . . . . . . . . . .
B: (Chorus)          *She's got a ticket to ride,* . . . . . . . . . . . . . . . . . . . . . . . . . . . .
                  . . . . . . . . . . . . . . . . . . . . . . . . . . . . . . . . . . . . . . . . . . .
                  . . . . . . . . . . . . . . . . . . . . . . . . . . . . . . . . . . . . . . . . . . .
                  . . . . . . . . . . . . . . . . . . . . . . . .
(Coda)               *My baby don't care. (repeat and fade)* . . . . . . . . . . . . . . . .

This form and its variants often give a powerful sense of climax and movement to a song as it mounts through the three important sections.

## The Rhythm of the Lyric

The term "rhythm" is applied to both speech and music. It is perhaps the greatest force unifying lyric, melody, and harmony. The beat and tempo of a song's music should agree with the theme in the title and words. The patterns of a song's rhythm may serve as a template on which the notes of the melody are matched with words or syllables of the lyric. Developing music and words that work together in interesting rhythms is half the battle of writing a great song.

Good song lyrics must be natural-sounding and memorable, so it helps to know about natural speech patterns. Examining the rhythms of song lyrics you admire can sharpen your ability to shape a phrase. In "The Sounds of Silence" by Paul Simon, the rhythm of the lyrics and music create a steady, insistent beat. The natural accents of the first two lines fall in a very regular pattern. (The "u" stands for "unaccented;" the " - " for "accented.")

```
    -   u   -   u    -   u   -
   Hel-lo dark-ness my old friend
u    -   u -   u   -   u   -
I've come to talk with you a - gain
```

Here's how the accented syllables of the lyrics correspond with the musical beats of each measure. The unaccented syllables fall on the offbeats.

| 1 | 2 | 3 | 4 | 1 | 2 | 3 | 4 |
|---|---|---|---|---|---|---|---|
| ( | -) (u | -) (u | -) (u | - ) | | | |
| | Hel-lo | dark-ness my old | | friend | | | |
| 1 | 2 | 3 | 4 | 1 | 2 | 3 | 4 |
| ( u | - ) (u | - )(u - ) (u | | - ) | | | |
| I've | come to talk with you a - | | | gain | | | |

Line two shows the pattern clearly: da-dum da-dum da-dum da-dum. This alternating pattern of unaccented and accented syllables is the fundamental rhythm of English speech and the basic rhythm (or meter) of all poetry and song lyrics written in English. A single beat (û–) is called an *iamb,* and song lyrics must have an iambic feeling in order to sound natural. Very regular iambic lyrics like those of "The Sounds of Silence" and "Say, Has Anybody Seen My Sweet Gypsy Rose" match well with the insistent beat of the music. This creates power and movement in the song and makes it easy to remember.

## Iambic Rhythm

Some songwriters use iambic rhythm in a pattern that alternates with the musical beats of a measure. This lyrical technique is a natural choice if you are working with a strongly syncopated melody. The combination can give your song a terrific feeling of excitement and suspense. Elton John makes use of this rhythmic interplay in the opening measures of his hit "Rocket Man."

| 1 | 2 | 3 | 4 |
|---|---|---|---|
| *(u  -)* | *(u  -)* | *(u  -)* | *(u  -)* |
| *She packed* | *my bags* | *last night* | *pre-flight* |

Here again, the iambic rhythm in the lyrics is plain and simple: da-dum da-dum da-dum da-dum. But both lyrics and melody are featured on the offbeats in an almost pounding syncopation. Each two-word phrase seems to surge toward each new musical beat of the measure in an alternating pattern of tension and momentum. This very regular, soaring effect of this rhythmic pattern sets the stage nicely for the song's theme, a futuristic portrait of the life of a lonely astronaut.

## Trochaic Rhythm

Sometimes the basic iambic pattern is reversed to produce what, in poetic terms, is called *trochaic* pattern: dum-da dum-da dum-da dum-da. This rhythm is often used to add punch to a song's chorus or hook, as in "Take It to the Limit" by the Eagles.

| 1 | 2 | 3 | 1 | 2 | 3 |
|---|---|---|---|---|---|
| *(-  u)* | | *(-  u )* | *(-  u)* | | |
| *Take it* | | *to the* | *limit* | | |

Here the *trochee* (pronounced troh-key) is the underlying metrical figure. It provides emphasis on the downbeats of the hook phrase. This effect is repeated throughout the chorus of the song. Michael Jackson's number one hit "Beat It" uses an even simpler trochaic pattern to emphasize the song's title and hook repeatedly in the chorus.

| 1 | 2 | 3 | 4 | 1 | 2 | 3 | 4 |
|---|---|---|---|---|---|---|---|
| (- u) | | | | (- u) | | | |
| Beat it. | | | | Beat it. | | | |

Notice how the accented/unaccented pattern of the trochee in both examples lends itself well to the commands "take it" and "beat it." Many other hit songs use this rhythm to stress important words, including Bobby Hebb's version of "Sunny," Smokey Robinson's classic "My Girl," and "Daniel" by Elton John. Try building your own song around a title or important lyric line using this underlying rhythmic pattern. This will help you to create a very positive and memorable chorus.

### Spondaic Rhythm

Songwriters sometimes choose evenly stressed syllables to create emphasis. Here, the basic metrical figure is called a *spondee* and is notated as (- -). Using spondaic rhythms can give a lyric a feeling of fullness and importance. Songwriters often employ this rhythmic technique when working with an uptune or power ballad that features a simple, accented, or sustained melody. Spondaic rhythm is very apparent in the opening measure of Joe Cocker's version of "You Are So Beautiful to Me."

| 1 | 2 | 3 | 4 | 1 | 2 | 3 | 4 |
|---|---|---|---|---|---|---|---|
| | (- | -) | (- | - u u) | | | |
| | You | are | so | beautiful | | | |

The underlying rhythm is clear: dum-dum dum-dum and the accented beats of both the melody and lyrics correspond with the musical beats of the first measure. The message of the lyric comes across strong and simple. Just a few notable recordings that feature the spondaic pattern are Mouth and MacNeal's "How Do You Do?," Cher's "Half Breed," and the J. Geils Band's "Love Stinks." Try writing a driving uptune with a spondaic hook of your own. It helps if you stick to short phrases to make the heavy accents sound both distinctive and natural.

There are many variations on the three basic rhythmic patterns described above: iambic, trochaic, and spondaic. These include larger figures like (û û -), (û - û), (- - û), and (- û -). Sometimes the overall rhythm of the music may suggest a particular style of song and the lyric often contains the same flavor. The hard, funky rhythm of Stevie Wonder's "Living for the City" makes a nice match with the urban imagery and street philosophy of its lyrics. The rhythmic Caribbean flavor of Harry Nilsson's version of "Coconut" is echoed in the lyric: "You put the lime in the coconut."

## Rhyme in the Lyric

As you are writing a song, the decisions you make about rhyme can help you determine what form the song should take or vice versa. You will find it helpful to be familiar with the rhyming patterns of your own songs, as well as those used by other songwriters. This should give you many options for developing rhyme in your lyrics.

The form that you choose for a particular song is one of the factors that determines where your rhymes should be placed. As a general rule, rhymes occur at the end of alternating lines of lyric, at the ends of sections, or in the song's hook. Once you have a good idea what the sections of your song will be like, you'll be able to see where the rhymes should go. In this way, rhyme is used to frame and fortify the form of the song itself.

### Typical Rhyme Schemes

For the purpose of outlining rhyme schemes, writers use letters to label the rhyming pairs. Don't be confused by the fact that we've already used letters to label the song sections that make up a song form, as in ABAB (verse/chorus/verse/chorus). Here is a traditional rhyming pattern, the ABCB form.

| | |
|---|---|
| *Give my regards to Broadway,* | *A* |
| *Remember me to Herald Square;* | *B* |
| *Tell all the gang at Forty-second Street* | *C* |
| *That I will soon be there.* | *B* |
| | |
| *Whisper of how I'm yearning* | *D* |
| *To mingle with the old-time throng;* | *E* |
| *Give my regards to old Broadway* | *F* |
| *And say that I'll be there e'er long.* | *E* |

Lines two and four of the first verse rhyme, with "Square" and "there," and the same lines rhyme in the second verse with "throng" and "long." Notice how the last word in each verse is a rhyme. This is the basic rhyming form of American popular music and of centuries of English and American poetry. It is the rhyme scheme of the English ballad, the same ballad that gives us our modern-day term for a song with a slow tempo.

Sometimes this pattern is reversed, and the first and third lines rhyme, while the second and fourth do not, as in Cat Stevens's version of the old hymn "Morning Has Broken."

| | |
|---|---|
| *Morning has broken* | A |
| *Like the first morning,* | B |
| *Blackbird has spoken* | A |
| *Like the first bird.* | C |

Sometimes lyricists choose to rhyme all the alternating lines to create the ABAB pattern as is common in many hymns and Christmas carols:

| | |
|---|---|
| *Angels we have heard on high,* | A |
| *Sweetly singing o'er the plain,* | B |
| *And the mountains in reply,* | A |
| *Echoing the joyous strain.* | B |

This type of rhyme scheme is quite straightforward and is usually used only with repeated phrases in popular music. Even fully repeated phrases are said to rhyme.

| | |
|---|---|
| *'Cause we are living in a material world.* | A |
| *And I am a material girl.* | B |
| *You know that we are living in a material world.* | A |
| *And I am a material girl.* | B |

A couplet is two consecutive rhyming lines, and this is the basis of the AABB pattern:

| | |
|---|---|
| *It was twenty years ago today,* | A |
| *Sergeant Pepper taught the band to play,* | A |
| *They've been going in and out of style,* | B |
| *But they're guaranteed to bring a smile.* | B |

This rhyme pattern is reminiscent of many children's rhymes and can give song lyrics an old-time, or innocent, feeling.

Because song form has changed in recent years, songwriters have experimented with many new and successful rhyme schemes, creating countless variations of these basic patterns. Sometimes the music and the rhythm of a song are so strong that a songwriter may choose to exclude rhyme from a particular section of the song, as in the opening verse of "Proud Mary":

| | |
|---|---|
| *Left a good job in the city,* | A |
| *Workin' for The Man ev'ry night and day,* | B |
| *And I never lost one minute of sleepin',* | C |
| *Worryin' 'bout the way things might have been.* | D |

The trend today, however, is toward song lyrics with elaborate rhyme schemes and, as a result, contemporary lyrics allow for looser rhyming.

## Imperfect Rhymes

An imperfect rhyme is formed by words that sound similar enough to give the effect of rhyming, yet are not true rhymes like "kite" and "night." Instead, the rhyming words usually have similar vowels and identical consonants, as in "love" and "prove" or similar consonant endings and identical vowels, as in "cat" and "sad." Used judiciously, imperfect rhymes can make a powerful contribution to your song lyric. A classic use of imperfect rhyme occurs in the first lines of Charles K. Harris's historic hit, "After the Ball."

> *After the ball is over, after the break of* **morn,**
> *After the dancers' leaving, after the stars are* **gone;**
> *Many a heart is aching, if you could read them* all;
> *Many the hopes that have vanished, after the* ball.

Here, lines one and two rhyme, with the words "morn," and "gone." While these words do not form a true, or perfect, rhyme (like "all" and "ball" in lines three and four), they are similar sounding enough to create a strong rhyming effect.

Don't overuse imperfect rhymes in the lyric because they can take away from the power of the song's form and the impact of the lyric itself. Too many imperfect rhymes can make a song lyric difficult for others to remember. It's important to create strong imperfect rhymes by using vowel sounds or consonant endings that are similar. The hard consonant sounds of *d, t, b, p, c,* and *g,* usually work well together in imperfect rhymes, as in "led" and "get," or "log" and "dock." *F* and *v* are also a good consonant pair for imperfect rhymes, as in "leave" and "grief." Combinations of related consonants can also make effective rhymes, as in "mess" and "let's" or "carve" and "off." Although vowels are more often identical in imperfect rhymes, related vowel sounds like *oh, uh, ah,* and even *eh* can make for interesting imperfect rhymes. In this case, the consonants must be identical, as in "fun" and "on" or "sun" and "men."

## Internal Rhyme

Internal rhymes do not occur at the end of a line, but create rhyme from within a line. An internal rhyme could be as simple as that in "My Baby Does the Hanky-Panky" or "Tonight's the Night." Sometimes an internal rhyme works to emphasize a true rhyme at the end of the line. Think of Curtis Mayfield's chorus to "Superfly":

> *Super***fly,**
> *Gonna make your fortune* **by** *and* **by.**

Many times internal rhyme can serve to make a line sound interesting and novel. Internal rhyme helps emphasize the unusual title of Mayfield's "Freddie's Dead":

> Fred*die's* **dead**,
> *That's what I* **said**.

The Beatles created some very novel effects with internal rhyme, as in the unusual first phrase of "I Am the Walrus":

> *I am* **he** *as you are* **me** *as you are* **we**
> *And* **we** *are all together.*

An even subtler use of internal rhyming can be made from line to line of your song lyric. There's a memorable internal rhyme of this kind in the first two lines of "Love Is a Rose":

> *Love is a* **rose,** *but you better not pick it*
> *Only* **grows** *when it's on the vine,*

By using a strong internal rhyme on the second beats of both the first and second line, the songwriter has set off the phrases "Love is a rose," and "Only grows." The rhyme not only sounds good, it emphasizes the important metaphor and theme of the song and makes it memorable.

### Rhymes in Repetition

Repetitive rhyme schemes can give song lyrics a comic effect. Think of the obvious repetitions of the typical limerick form (AABBA).

> *There was an old man of Nantucket*    A
> *Who kept all his money in a bucket.*    A
> *His daughter, named Nan,*    B
> *Ran off with a man.*    B
> *And as for the bucket, Nan tuk it.*    A

Repetetive rhyming patterns and internal rhyme may also be used to create a more serious tone, and add a feeling of importance to song lyrics. Heavy rhyming can add a lot of movement to a song, especially when used in uptunes.

>       B         A
> *Hello, Mary* **Lou**—*Goodbye* **heart.**    A
>      B                B
> *Sweet Mary* **Lou,** *I'm so in love with* **you.**    B
>   B      B      A
> *I* **knew,** *Mary* **Lou,** *we'd never* **part,**    A
>       B      A
> *So, hello, Mary* **Lou**—*Goodbye* **heart.**    A

Here, the simple ABAA rhyme scheme and the many related internal rhymes cleverly support the simple message of the lyric. Perhaps most important, strong rhyming can do a lot to make your song lyric memorable.

As you are developing rhymes, be sure that they support the meaning of each phrase in a direct and natural way. It's better to use a simple rhyming pattern or resort to imperfect rhymes than to have the meaning of the lyric become tortured or unclear because of the demands of an overly intricate rhyme scheme. The best way to avoid this problem is to develop the individual lyric phrases and their rhymes as part of the same process. If it seems impossible to rhyme a line in a natural way, try another line, or come back to it when more of the lyric are written to see if it's really worth working on. Don't stymie yourself with a hook or repeating phrase in a rhyming position that is difficult to find rhymes for. When you come up with an important phrase, make sure you can think of at least three familiar words that rhyme with it before you try to work it into the lyric. A good rhyming dictionary is a wonderful resource. If you don't have one already, buy one and see if it doesn't help stimulate your ability to create solid rhyme schemes.

## Imagery

In the short space of a song, a songwriter must portray the theme of the lyric in an interesting and concise way. All song lyrics use images to give the listener a clear picture of the overall story or message. By using images, the songwriter illustrates the story, rather than relying only on emotions and opinions to get the message across. In Elton John's "Daniel" the image of the "red taillights" of the departing plane and "Daniel waving good-bye" are perceived by the speaker, Daniel's younger brother (or sister). These touching images illustrate the main event of the song as stated in the first line: "Daniel's riding tonight on a plane." Thus, when the speaker states that "I miss Daniel," it does not seem like an out-of-context cliché, but rather the likely result of a very real separation of family members. Almost everyone has experienced an important good-bye scene that included the vanishing red taillights of a plane or car. This familiar image was cleverly identified by the songwriter as a universal symbol of parting and personal loss.

Sometimes a songwriter lists related images to portray the theme of the lyrics. In the George and Ira Gershwin classic "They Can't Take That Away from Me," the speaker remembers the many familiar visions and events of a past romance. Images like "the way you wear your hat" and "the way you sip your tea" are touchingly simple and specific. In fact, it is the speaker's remembrance of the images themselves that constitutes the song's theme: "They can't take that away from me." Most people have had similar daily visions of someone they care for.

In most songs, a writer returns to the images that are important to the development of the story. In Harry Chapin's "Taxi" we learn in the first line that "it was raining hard in Frisco." The writer brings in a logically related image in the second verse when the speaker says, "It's a shame you ruined your gown in the rain." Thus, the rainy city night intensifies the drama of the chance reunion of the taxi driver and the well-to-do woman. Here, the rain-soaked gown serves to illustrate her paradoxical life of unhappiness and success. As a general rule, don't just use an image because it is interesting or clever. Good imagery should work to illustrate the theme of the lyric and be woven into the song's story in a natural and meaningful way.

Songs of different popular musical styles, like pop, rock, or country, often incorporate their own characteristic imagery. For instance, many teen-oriented pop songs use images from settings familiar to today's youth culture. Dance clubs, car rides, home, and school provide images like the car radio, the telephone, and blue jeans—familiar and meaningful images in the life of the teenaged listener.

Sometimes a songwriter chooses an unfamiliar image to illustrate the main theme of a song. Here, it is important to explain the image so that it seems familiar to the listener by the time the song ends. In the Tony Orlando and Dawn hit version of "Tie a Yellow Ribbon Round the Ole Oak Tree," the main image is unfamiliar, and even obscure, at the beginning of the song. During the course of the song, we come to understand the special significance of the image: a woman's signal to a released prisoner that their love affair is still intact. By the time the speaker brings this image to mind for the last time, we are fully familiar with its meaning. This image is the most memorable part of the song, primarily because it is included in the title and the much-repeated hook and it expresses the song's main theme.

## Musical Language—The Sung Word

Language is the lyricist's only tool, but it is really the sung word, or musical language, that a lyricist uses to create a song, even when the lyrics are written before the music. Any good lyricist knows the physical limitations of the human voice and the nature of language when it is sung rather than spoken. Short vowels (like the *i* in the word lit) are not as pleasant sounding as long vowels (like the *i* in light); a seasoned lyricist will consciously work to avoid them whenever possible. The length of a line of lyric is often limited by the breath control of a vocalist, so the lyricist keeps the lines short enough to sing as one phrase, or provides a logical place in the line for the performer to breathe. These are just a few of the technical considerations that the lyricist has in mind when writing. But don't let the rules stifle your imagination.

The best thing to remember about writing is that your words are not carved in stone. Paper and pens are easy to come by, and many a popular song lyric went through several changes before the song's actual release. Your ear should tell you when a lyric doesn't fit the music. No matter how wonderful you think a particular line is, if it doesn't work well with the song's melody, it is no good. The benefit is that when the lyrics do work well with the music, you have met the greatest challenge of writing a good song.

## Figures of Speech

Song lyrics, like literature, use figures of speech to provide nuances of meaning to the facts as they unfold. Even the simplest and most straightforward lyrics contain figures of speech, as do most of the conversations we hear each day. Song lyrics that do not contain figures of speech will read like newspaper articles, as a simple statement of facts, with no double meanings. Below are a few of the techniques that lyricists favor most. Your awareness of their construction, and the power they add to the work of others, should benefit your material.

### Metaphor

A *metaphor* is simply a way of defining one idea by saying it is another. Most metaphors are linked with "is," "am," or "are." In the Linda Ronstadt hit "Love Is a Rose," the title/first line is a simple metaphor. We know that love is not literally a rose, but the characteristics they share are explained in the lyric. Both only grow when they're "on the vine." This statement applies literally to the rose, but the listener must infer the second meaning, that love cannot sustain itself if it is removed from its natural, nurtured state. This powerful metaphor is the foundation for the entire lyric, and lends an almost mystical tone of truth to the song's message. In the Kenny Rogers/Dolly Parton hit "Islands in the Stream," we learn that the title is a metaphor for the character and relationship of the two speakers— "islands in the stream, that is what we are." Dolly Parton uses a fascinating metaphor in the second line of her hit "9 to 5"—"pour myself a cup of ambition." Here, coffee as ambition is an implied metaphor.

There are many examples of metaphors, large and small, in today's song lyrics. Get used to picking them out of the lyrics you hear, and you will be able to incorporate them smoothly into your own lyrics. You need not build the whole lyric of your song around a metaphor to make it effective. As long as the metaphor draws comparisons that are relatively clear, you can feel free to use the figure of speech at any point in your lyrics.

### Simile

A simile defines an idea by associating it with another. Here the two ideas are compared with the linking words "like" or "as." Songs that use a simile as the main theme for the lyric include Madonna's "Like a Virgin" and Paul Simon's "Loves Me Like a Rock." Another Simon hit, "Bridge over Troubled Water," features the simile "like a bridge over troubled water, I will lay me down." When a lyric is built around a simile, it often features the figure in the title.

Like a metaphor, a simile need not be the guiding light of the lyrical theme. As long as the association you are making is clear, similes can be very effectively woven into your lyric. Think of the song classic "Misty," in which the speaker states, "I'm as helpless as a kitten up a tree," and, in the next line, feels "like I'm clinging to a cloud." These unrelated similes both illustrate the speaker's feeling of elevation and helplessness, the underlying theme of the song. Yet here, their meaning stands by itself and requires no further development. The general rule is, if you choose a familiar image for your simile, with familiar connotations, it can stand alone. If you choose an unfamiliar image for your simile, then you've got some explaining to do.

Another kind of simile is the *comparative simile,* which uses the linking word "than" to compare two ideas. The classic "Younger Than Springtime" uses this device in its title, but this figure can be very useful if it is woven carefully into the song lyric itself. The song theme from the motion picture *Love Story* uses a comparative simile in the second line of the lyric—"The sweet love story that is older than the sea." Or think of the repeated use in Paul Simon's "El Condor Pasa": "I'd rather be a sparrow than a snail," "I'd rather be a forest than a tree." As these comparative similes accumulate, a pattern becomes clear. The speaker prefers to be associated with images in nature that symbolize the breadth and freedom of the human soul. This can be very effective in your own lyrics but again, be sure the meaning is clear.

### Personification

Personification is the giving of human qualities to an idea or a non-human object. The Gershwin classic "Love Walked In," Ann Ronell's "Willow Weep for Me," and Hank Snow's country hit "Hello Love" are clear examples of personification used as the main theme of a song lyric. Prince's hit "When Doves Cry" makes a powerful and intriguing use of this technique.

Personification may be woven into song lyrics. In the second verse of the forties classic "Twilight Time," there is a memorable personification of the skyscape at sunset: "fingers of night will soon surrender the setting sun." In Billy Joel's "Baby Grand," the piano is powerfully personified with the word "she" as his best friend and lover: "when I'm lonely she comes through, she's the only one who can, my baby grand." When using personifications, be sure you choose objects and ideas that are important enough to warrant human characteristics.

## Hyperbole

Hyperbole is just exaggeration. Paul Simon's "50 Ways to Leave Your Lover" is a clever use of hyperbole. Sting's "Every Breath You Take" makes powerful use of exaggeration to prove a point. We don't really believe that the singer will be literally watching the subject's every breath and move, but it suggests the intensity of the speaker's obsession.

## Understatement

Understatement is another way a lyricist can drive a point home. Here, an important idea is paradoxically de-emphasized to make it stand out. A classic example is the song "I Remember You" by Johnny Mercer and Victor Schertzinger. In the last verse the speaker states that after his death, "when the angels ask me to recall the thrill of them all," he answers in the brilliant understatement, "Then I shall tell them I remember you."

## Alliteration

Alliteration (the repetition of consonant sounds) is an effective way to make lyrics catchy and memorable. Though many song titles contain alliteration, like "Tea for Two," you will also notice its use in almost every lyric you hear. "Are You Ever Coming Back," as recorded by the Human League, uses a strong alliteration in the first line: "The sun that's shining through the shattered window." Here the repetition of the "sh" sound gives a musical quality to the words. In the next line, the consonant "c" is used for the same effect: "Is breaking into colors in the car." Alliteration is just one way of tying a line of lyric together and making it sound polished.

## Assonance

Assonance is the repetition of vowel sounds, and it has the same unifying and musical effect on language that is achieved with alliteration. David Bowie's "Day-In Day-Out" makes a strong use of assonance in the chorus: "Day-in day-out, stay-in fade-out." Here, the repetition of the long *a* sound ties together the hook and chorus in an almost chantlike pattern that is hard to forget. Like alliteration, assonance can help to make your lyrics memorable.

The figures of speech and poetic techniques discussed here are popularly used in today's song lyrics. There are no rules for how many times you can use a figure of speech in your own lyrics, although, as with rhyming, you don't ever want to twist the sense of the text to fit a figure that you like. Let your ear be the judge of whether a figure is appropriate or not. A careless or overly complex use of figures of speech can make a lyric sound hazy or insincere. Used properly and naturally, they can deepen the meaning, as well as the artistic value, of your song lyrics.

## Matching the Lyric with the Music

The value of a song lyric can not be assessed until it is matched with the melody. Whether you are a lyricist collaborating with a composer or crafting your own music and words, this stage of the songwriting process is perhaps the most important of all. Remember, matching music with lyric is just like making a good marriage: there are sure to be some compromises made along the way.

Your first task is to be sure that the rhythm of the melody and that of the lyric match. The music and words should also work together to create a complementary tone throughout the song. A humorous lyric, for example, obviously is not going to complement a sober melody. There are a few techniques that can help you to create subtle agreements of tone in word and music, chief among them is *word-painting*.

### Word-Painting

Word-painting is one technique that the lyricist can only employ when the melody (or sometimes the harmony) of the song is already completed. With word-painting, the lyricist illustrates the movements of the music itself in words. A classic example of word-painting occurs in the 5th Dimension hit "Up, Up and Away." As the melody of the first line soars up the octave, the lyric points out this movement with the words "Up, up and away." In a similar way, the lyric of the Blood, Sweat and Tears hit "Spinning Wheel" states that "What goes up must come down," as the melody correspondingly moves up and down in pitch. A more subtle use of word-painting occurs in the Merle Haggard hit "Blues Stay Away from Me." The first note of the melody is a minor or "blue" note, corresponding the the word "blues." At the end of Bread's hit song "If," the lyric states that the two main characters "will simply fly away." Here, the melody goes up the scale, and the song itself seems to fade away into its own musical heights.

A natural use of this technique in your own song material is not always obvious to the listener, but the subliminal effects of word-painting are powerful indeed.

### The Final Stages

The process of matching the words and music is often where songwriters get bogged down. This is, after all, one of the final stages of songwriting and perhaps the most difficult. If you're having trouble getting a particular line to fit, see if the lyric or melody can be changed to make a better match without compromising the meaning or musical integrity of the song itself. If you find that this is not possible, don't waste time trying to put a square peg in a round hole. It's better to work on something else or start the lyric from scratch than to try to get words and music together that are not well suited to begin with.

Many songwriters will leave the lyric or melody alone for days, weeks, or even months, and make a fresh start later when the ideas have had some time to gel. You may find that a different tempo or feel is just the thing to provide a new common ground for words and music. Maybe you started out writing a ballad that works much better as an uptune. Even though you've been working very closely with your material, there comes a time when it helps to get a larger perspective on the song. Listen to a tape of your performance of an unfinished song, or have someone you know and trust play or sing parts of the song for you, so you can hear it from the listener's point of view. Above all, don't be too critical of your work in its formative stages. There will be plenty of time to revise and shape your lyric with the music after the main body of the song exists.

# 7

# Songwriting Methods

*If I am trying to write a melodic song hit, I let Richard Rodgers get his tune first. Then I take the most distinctive melodic phrase in his tune, and work on that. Next I try to find the meaning of that phrase and to develop a euphonic set of words to fit it.*

—Lorenz Hart

*There are no magic formulae. . . . There are no hidden charts either.*

—Oscar Hammerstein II

*Whatever patterns songwriters have you can pretty much eliminate in my case. I've done everything from write a song in 10 minutes to write two verses of a song and five years later finally come up with a third verse, and all extremes in the middle. I've been writing when I was miserable and I've written when I was happy. I've written when I was unhappy in love; I've written when I was happy in love. I've written on the road, off the road, in a studio, not in a studio. So that even in the search I couldn't really find a system.*

—John Sebastian

## Lyric-First Approach

Many songs are developed from an existing lyric or part of a lyric. This songwriting approach is a natural for a lyricist (although many lyricists create the words to a song only after the melody is written). Many singer/songwriters also have a natural feeling for words and create the lyric before they write the music. The lyric alone can determine certain aspects of the song as a whole. In this way, the lyric-first approach can make the process of creating the song's music more clear-cut. By making the task of the composer more defined, the lyricist can smooth the way for an easy collaboration (although be aware that some composers work best using the melody-first approach).

A completed lyric contains clearly identifiable sections and in this way establishes the basic form of the song. The lyric also contains the hook and establishes the song's main theme and overall tone. Clearly, the rhythm of the lyric determines the basic rhythmic pattern of the melody. Important phrases and rhymes also provide guideposts for melodic and harmonic highlights. Here's an example of the lyric of a simple song that is ready to be set to music.

> *Verse:*      *If it's lovin' you want,*
>                   *Well, you know I'm around,*
>                   *If you just want someone to talk to,*
>                   *I won't make a sound.*
>                   *If you just want to use me,*
>                   *As a shoulder to cry on.*
>                   *Or a shadow to follow you around,*
>
> *Chorus:*     *I'm available*
>                   *And my intentions are good*
>                   *I'm available*
>                   *And it should be understood*
>                   *That you're the only one who can see*
>                   *My availability.*

The lines are short, and the natural rhythm and aggressive tone of the lyric suggests a power ballad or uptune. The rhyme scheme is regular, ABCBDEB for the verse and ABABCC for the chorus. This suggests that the melody and harmony should highlight the rhymes in lines two, four, and seven of the verse and lines two and four, and five and six of the chorus, respectively. The hook phrase, "I'm available," is repeated twice in the chorus and should be emphasized by the melody, perhaps by repetition. The syllables "I'm a-" naturally suggest a pickup, with "-vailable" beginning on a strong downbeat. The unfinished sentence at the end of the verse is completed by the hook line of the chorus, suggesting a high unresolved harmony which moves to a strong tonic chord. Thus, the music might go something like this:

# I'm Available

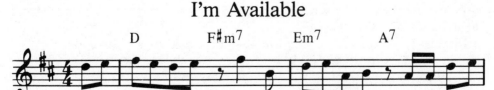

As you can see, there are often clues in a song lyric that can help shape the music, but this approach demands that the composer be sensitive to these guidelines in a creative way. Many other musical settings would be appropriate to the lyric in this example. Try writing your own melody and chords for this lyric or use one of your own lyrics to explore this method of songwriting.

Keep in mind that even though the lyric may be complete, it will eventually be revised to highlight or complement certain elements of the music in the later stages of the songwriting process. Remember, the lyric depends on the musical elements of the song for its artistic value, and it should be flexible to the demands of the music.

## Hook-First Approach

Some songwriters start out with nothing more than the words of the title or the hook of a song and this naturally helps develop the rhythm and perhaps the melody of the chorus. For example, if you come up with the idea, "I'm gonna get you in the end" as a hook, you should have a good idea of how you intend to set this phrase rhythmically to give it the desired impact. This idea would naturally be shaped by the genre, tempo, and theme of the song. Here are a few possibilities:

Continuing with this example, the lyric you choose for a title or hook might also strongly suggest a melody. In this lyric the speaker's confidence suggests a power ballad treatment:

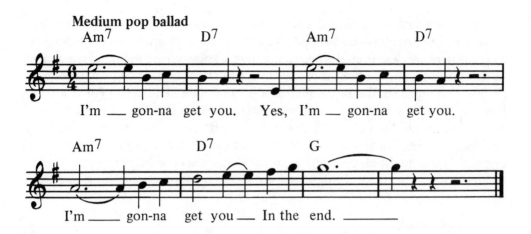

Here the simple, powerful melody merely repeats for the first two lines, "I'm gonna get you," until the final phrase, "In the end." The melody climaxes on a sustained high note on the final word, lending a feeling of optimism or hope.

Perhaps the speaker's aggressive statement suggests a feeling of mounting tension and force, and with each new reiteration of the phrase "I'm gonna get you," the melody line is raised in pitch. On the phrase "In the end," the drop of an octave emphasizes the finality of the entire statement.

You can probably think of more ways to express the message of this particular hook in a melody. Try using this approach with some of your own hooks. This is a great way to ensure that the melody and lyric are working well together during the song's important hook section.

Sometimes a hook inspires the songwriter to create the harmony of the song next. Since the hook is often repeated in the verse or chorus, certain aspects of its placement are clear from the beginning. If you know where the hook will repeat in the song, and how often, it is easy to begin shaping the song's harmony. A phrase that suggests the beginning of a general idea like "Let's hear it for the boy" or "Beat it" will probably be featured best in the first line of a chorus section. This should be a climactic point in the harmonic movement of the song and begin a new harmonic progression that carries through to the end of the chorus. Thus, the hook phrase, "I got you," suggests the beginning of an idea to kick off the chorus and might inspire a pop harmony something like this:

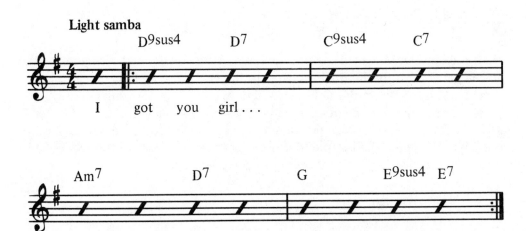

Certain hooks, like "Until it's time for you to go" or "The best of my love," suggest the end of an idea and might work best in the last line of the chorus or the verse. Of course, rules are meant to be bent, as with the hook of Madonna's hit "Like a Virgin." This phrase sounds like the end of a sentence, but is featured as the first line of the chorus. (If you bend the rules in this way, be sure the last lines of the verse prepare the listener for the important hook line at the beginning of the chorus.) More often, this type of phrase is featured at the end of the chorus or verse and require a full, round harmony in the last line to emphasize its importance. Sometimes an extended harmonic progression for this final line really does the trick, as in the last line of Aretha Franklin's song, "Until You Come Back to Me (That's What I'm Gonna Do)." Here, the hook line is fairly long, and the final chords of the chorus are correspondingly full and decisive.

Sometimes the hook is repeated several times in the chorus, and the harmony of the chorus does not resolve, but carries directly back to the verse section of the song. Some songwriters resolve the harmony of the last chorus with the help of a coda section. More often, the recording simply fades out repeating the hook and the harmonic resolution. This is usually appropriate for a shorter hook phrase like "in the end." Here the last two lines of the chorus should be harmonized so that the last two measures allow a smooth repeat and fade.

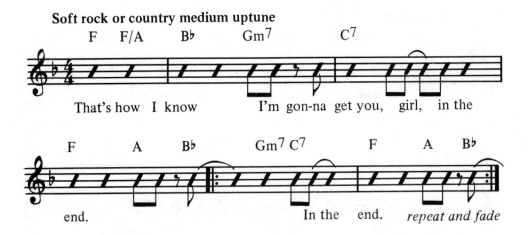

If you are a guitarist or pianist, building a song from its hook may come quite naturally to you. Try harmonizing a few of your own hooks. This approach may really help you to frame the vital hook phrase with strong and natural harmonies.

## Melody-First Approach

Many singers and instrumentalists begin to write a song after they have a melody line, or part of a melody, in mind. Sometimes only a few notes are enough to inspire a songwriter to create a song. Many melodies are simply the development of one or two phrases in patterns of variation. For example, Bruce Springsteen's "Pink Cadillac" repeats the step-wise melody of the hook phrase many times during the course of the song, in several variations.

The melody-first approach is common in collaborative songwriting situations, when a composer or instrumentalist completes the song's music before turning it over to a lyricist. Many melodies imply their own harmony so strongly that no alternative harmonization seems appropriate. This is particularly true of blues and country songs, where traditional harmonies are key to the success of a given song within its genre. This may seem like a constraint to the songwriter. But, once comfortable with the rules of a chosen musical style, a good songwriter views these harmonic guidelines as dependable friends that give a familiar, and even classic, sound to the material. The most common mistake a beginning songwriter makes is to put overcomplicated or obscure harmony to a melody that is crying out for simplicity.

When one section of the song's melody is complete, it can suggest a lot about the rhythm and harmony of a song. These musical elements may be added soon after the melody takes shape, and sometimes it is hard to determine which elements actually are created first, because their interrelationships are so profound.

If you use the melody-first approach to songwriting, be sure to identify the aspects of the harmony that are logically suggested by the melody. Simply noting the most basic harmonic movement can really shorten the time you spend fine-tuning the song's harmonization. Usually just identifying the I chords, IV chords, and V chords will provide a basic harmonic sketch of a given song melody. Here's a fragment of a simple pop melody with its basic chord movements notated in this way:

After you've determined the basic harmony of the song, you can add some passing chords and substitutions to provide harmonic detail and interest.

Try using this approach to creating harmony with some of your melodies. You'll find that mapping out the overall harmonic movement is a great way to write harmonies that are logical and supportive of the melody.

A completed song melody has its own intrinsic rhythm that naturally suggests certain things about its overall rhythmic character. The rhythm of the melody is expressed mainly by a vocalist, and it makes sense for the songwriter to create the instrumental rhythms as the next likely step in the songwriting process. Thus, the rhythmic structure of the melody implies its own rhythmic complement. Here's the same pop melody that led to the creation of a harmonic structure in the previous example. Now, let's see what kind of rhythmic structures are implied. It could be powerful in a disco setting.

This melody also works well in a strong $\frac{4}{4}$ rock and roll rhythm.

Try playing one of your melodies in different settings. Which ones sound more natural? Which express the musical style that best characterizes your songwriting talents? Sometimes different instrumental rhythms can bring new life to a melody that seems difficult to harmonize. Deciding on the groove and feel of a melody is sometimes just the thing to give it a strong sense of personality. This can smooth the way for the development of the harmony and lyric.

## Harmony-First Approach

The harmony-first approach is a natural for guitarists and pianists who are typically familiar with chord progressions and harmonization. Even if you're not an expert on the piano or guitar, you may find this method of songwriting useful once you are familiar with some of the chord progressions used in popular music today. In creating the chords or harmony of a song, the songwriter must also map out the form of the song and make some decisions about its rhythm and beat.

Once you get to this stage, it is usually clear where the hook of the song will be, and what kind of melody and lyric will best complement the harmony.

Certain chord progressions suggest particular styles of music. When you hear the following progression you will probably be reminded of modern jazz or pop styles.

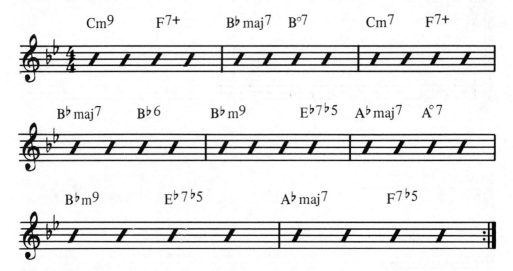

In the same way, it is difficult to play the next progression without hearing the echoes of bluegrass or old-time country music.

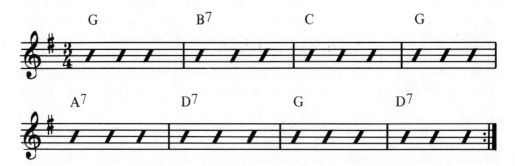

It is important to be familiar with the standard chord progressions used in the style of music you write. (In later chapters of this book that deal with particular musical styles including blues, rock, and country, you will find more examples of typical chord patterns.)

You will find it helpful to take the time to study the chord progressions of songs you particularly admire and pinpoint why the harmony is interesting or pleasing. A great way to get into the harmony-first approach to songwriting is to use the chords of a song you like as the basis for your own melody and lyric. Here are a few interesting chord patterns that you might want to use as the foundation for your writing.

This is a typical country harmony:

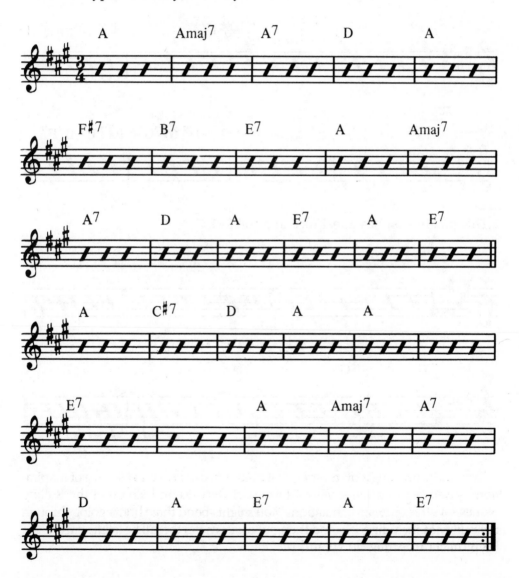

Try playing this classic blues progression and see what melodies come to mind.

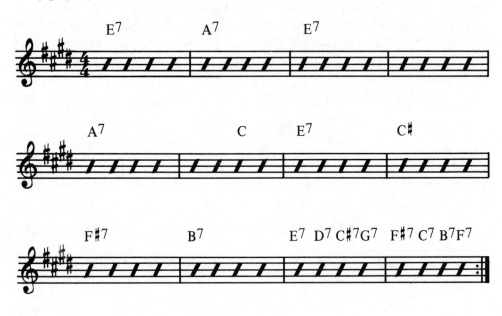

This progression has a real rock and roll feel:

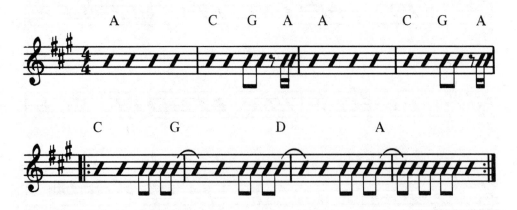

Even the great songwriters agree that imitation can be a great source of inspiration as well as being the sincerest form of flattery. Keith Richard of the Rolling Stones says this of creative imitation: "You might spend three hours going through the Buddy Holly songbook, and then out of nowhere, there'll be a little crash. . . . It's a matter of sitting down and playing."

## Rhythm/Riff-First Approach

The success of songs like "Stairway to Heaven," "Layla," and "Smoke on the Water" is due in part to the distinctive rhythmic instrumental introductions and the repetition of the instrumental motif throughout. These motifs are sometimes the kernel of a songwriting idea and are sufficient to inspire their own setting. Instrumentalist/songwriters sometimes develop a whole song from a rhythmic idea or riff that they particularly like. This is a natural approach if you play a rhythm instrument like the guitar, piano, or drums. Even a singer with a good musical imagination can devise an entire song from one rhythm or riff. Keep in mind that it takes a strong and interesting idea to spark the whole creative process of writing a song. Don't try this approach if you don't feel your riff or rhythm idea is distinctive or catchy.

A guitar riff might serve well as the lead-in to a dance-oriented rock song. A variation of this motif might be just the thing to punctuate the vocal line in the chorus of the song, in call-and-answer fashion.

You might find the rhythm/riff-first approach to songwriting works well for you, particularly if you are writing in genres that rely on groove and feel for their definition as a musical style. For this reason, disco, funk, and Latin music are naturally suited to this songwriting approach.

The sophistication of drum machines has opened up this songwriting method to many people who have a natural sense of rhythm yet do not play a rhythm instrument. Whatever medium you use to develop your rhythm ideas or riffs, even if it's simply pencil and paper, this approach can help you get a handle on the groove and feel of a song. It is one way to ground your material in the stylistic elements responsible for the catchy sound of popular music today.

## Collaboration

Many classic songs were the product of collaborative songwriting. In fact, collaboration was the most common songwriting method in the twenties, thirties, and forties. This is because many hits of the day were a product of the Broadway stage, where collaboration is a must. The lyricist was often responsible not only for the creation of song lyrics but for the script or "book" portion of the musical play. Teams such as Richard Rodgers and Lorenz Hart and George and Ira Gerswhin produced many successful pop songs from their Broadway hits.

Other songwriting partnerships were not concerned with the staged musical. Duke Ellington and Hoagy Carmichael collaborated with various lyricists to create their songs. In the fifties and sixties, the advent of the pop group and rock band fostered many new collaborative songwriting teams like John Lennon and Paul McCartney, Jerry Lieber and Mark Stoller, Gerry Goffin and Carole King, and Daryl Hall and John Oates. Sometimes teams include more than two collaborators, like Brian Holland, Lamont Dozier, and Eddie Holland, who wrote for the Four

Tops. Many times, a rock group may credit several of its members with the creation of a song, as with many of the hits of Genesis, the Human League, Anthrax, and Poison. Many bands found success writing in rehearsal or at jam sessions, making group songwriting more popular today than ever. Keith Richard remarks on his need for this kind of collaborative process: "Rarely do I write a song totally by myself. Even if I actually do write it by myself, I always like to have someone around just playing along with me, saying, 'Yeah, yeah.' I'm a band man, a group man. I can't sit there alone in a room and say, 'It's songwriting time, ding, ding, ding.' "

As you plan your own collaborations, decide early in the game who is going to do what and in what general order. This is the best way to ensure success. Although traditionally the music of a song is created before the lyric, many songs have been written by the opposite approach. Like any team sport, collaboration involves compromise, so keep your mind on making the best song possible and leave your ego at the door when you meet with your co-workers. If you don't like an idea that is proposed to you, or you feel that you are going in different directions, sometimes it's a good idea to work it out at another session. Your partner(s) probably have a viable reason for voicing a suggestion. If you don't value their judgement enough to agree on a solution to a specific problem, then maybe you are not suited for a partnership. Some people just aren't cut out to collaborate, as Graham Nash will attest: "To collaborate you have to let somebody into your mind and I'm not sure I want to do that." Eddie Money seems to feel the same way: "I do as much homework as possible on tunes before I get in the studio, so people can't touch anything. 'Cause these are my songs, my puppies, my babies. I don't like anybody getting too involved with me."

If you want to write songs in collaboration, take the time to develop good working habits together. Once you have established a general work pattern, you'll find collaboration to be a supportive and enjoyable way to create good material. As the saying goes, "Two heads are better than one."

# 8

# *The Tools of the Trade*

*Because the cost of rehearsal time with studio players was (and is) high, we began to prepare fairly detailed charts before going into the studio, sometimes with the help of one of the musicians on the date. The players would run down the tune a few times and then we'd start recording.*

—Donald Fagen

*When I was a senior in high school I had a little local band, and we went into a studio to cut a record. It was really fascinating. A few months later I bought the studio.*

—T-Bone Burnett

It's important to be able to communicate well with musicians who are playing or recording, or even just rehearsing, your songs. Most musicians read music to some extent, so it is helpful to write down the lyric, chords, and, if possible, the melody to get the best results from rehearsals or recording sessions. The next best thing to having a leadsheet or chord chart for your song is to have a clear tape recording of you singing or playing it. Unless your song is very complex, a tape recording should be enough to communicate your song to most musicians.

To make the most efficient use of your time in these situations, you should be aware of the fundamentals of reading and writing music. Musicians will appreciate whatever you can do to make their job easier and the sessions smoother, and they'll have more time to work on the fine points of your song.

No matter how good the musicians are, a tape recording or a leadsheet can only serve to familiarize them with your song. You'll have to work out the nuances of the song's rhythm and feel and the song arrangement during rehearsal. Have a clear idea of how you want your songs to sound, but be open to suggestions. Sometimes a seasoned musician can come up with some excellent touches.

## Songwriting by Ear

You'd be surprised to know how many of today's successful singer/songwriters do not play an instrument, or even write their songs down. Many of the great jazz and blues artists of yesterday did not use writing to communicate their songs and arrangements to others; instead, they learned by listening to each other. This method is still used by many pop and rock groups today. Wham's songwriter, George Michael ended his musical education in high school because he didn't feel that writing music or mastering a musical instrument was necessary to his songwriting career. He explains that "the melodies were all stuck in my head and writing them down seemed totally irrelevant." Yet by using a tape recorder, he has written some great song successes for Wham.

Musicians who are not very familiar with the names and symbols of notes and chords are said to play or sing "by ear." If you write your songs by ear or are a beginner at putting music down on paper, you'll benefit from the help of other musicians. You can handle the first step by writing out or typing the lyrics to the song. It's a good idea to leave a few blank lines above each line of the lyrics, so that you have room for the chord symbols later.

If you feel comfortable using a tape recorder, it can be a powerful songwriting tool. You can use the machine as an audio notepad, a mirror or sounding board to critically examine your own ideas, a way of communicating your ideas to a collaborator, to musicians working on your song, or even as a instrument to sell your song. Similarly, as good synthesizers, drum machines, sequencers, and MIDI devices and software are becoming more affordable, whole new avenues of musical experimentation and home recording are available to the songwriter.

## Reading and Writing Music

There's no mystery to reading and writing music, it's simply a matter of practice. If you already play an instrument, you are familiar with chords and their names, so you should be able to do your own chord charts. If you play or sing entirely by ear, you'll need some help writing your songs down. In either case, you should take some time to familiarize yourself with the accepted formats for the written song.

Here is a quick rundown on the rudiments of reading and writing. This section will not make you totally musically literate, but will refresh your memory if your last brush with music notation occurred when you played clarinet in the junior high school band. If you have no experience with written music, what follows will at least acquaint you with the terms and a few of the conventions.

This will make it easier for you to pick up this skill from books or from a friend or teacher.

## Music Notation

Music for any instrument or voice is written by placing notes on a staff of five lines and four spaces. The most common clef is called the treble or G clef, which places the pitch G on the second line.

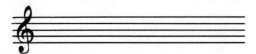

The rest of the lines and spaces represent these pitches. (Remember the grade-school mnemonic Every Good Boy Does Fine for the pitches on lines and the word FACE for those in the spaces?)

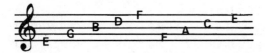

Temporary extensions of the staff, called *leger lines,* are used for notes that go below or above it. Notice the use of leger lines in this two-octave C major scale starting on middle C, which is the C note found closest to the middle of a piano keyboard.

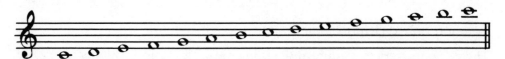

The notes in the C major scale above are called *natural* notes. Any one of these natural notes may be affected by a *sharp* or a *flat.* A sharp sign (#) in front of a note raises the pitch by one half-step, which is equal to the very next piano key, black or white, to the right of the natural note or one fret on a guitar. A flat sign ( ♭ ) lowers the pitch of the note that follows it by one half-step. When sharps and flats occur in the middle of a piece of music, they are called *accidentals.* Accidentals affect only the note to which they are applied, and any other note of the same pitch, for the duration of the measure. Here is an ascending *chromatic* scale, one including all the half steps, written with sharps.

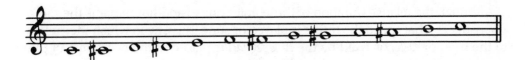

Now we'll come back down through all the same notes, notating them with flats.

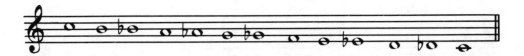

The symbol ( ♮ ) is a *natural* sign. It is an accidental, the same as a sharp or flat sign. It is used in front of a note that has been sharped or flatted by a previous accidental or by the *key signature* (explained below). Like an accidental sharp or flat, the natural affects only the pitch to which it is applied (it has no effect on the same note in other octaves) and lasts only for the duration of the measure in which it appears.

Sharps or flats appearing at the beginning of each line of music constitute a key signature. The key signature designates certain notes to be consistently sharped or flatted throughout the piece.

The key signature of D major tells you that all Fs are played as F-sharps and that all Cs are played as C-sharps. Similarly, in E-flat major, all Bs become B-flats, all Es are E-flats, and all As are A-flats. With each note's position on the staff denoting its pitch, you now need a way of expressing how long to hold each pitch. Let's look at the different types of notes, each of which stands for a different duration of sound.

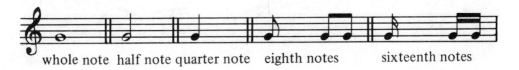

whole note   half note  quarter note     eighth notes          sixteenth notes

Although the relative duration of these notes one to another remains the same no matter at what speed the music is played or sung, the way in which they relate to the beat, or *meter,* is fixed by the *time signature* placed at the beginning of the music. It is the time signature that tells you how many beats there are per *measure* (or *bar*) and what kind of note constitutes one beat. The most common time signature is $\frac{4}{4}$. It is often referred to as common time and abbreviated as (**C**).

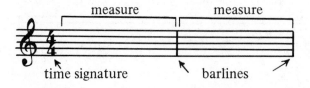

The top 4 of $\frac{4}{4}$ tells you that there are four beats in each measure. The bottom 4 means that a quarter note gets one beat. Here are a few measures of $\frac{4}{4}$ time with four quarter notes per measure.

In addition, each type of note has its corresponding *rest.* These stand for the equivalent time value of silence. This is what each kind of rest looks like.

Things could get pretty dull if we only wrote four quarter notes in every measure of $\frac{4}{4}$ time. If you think back to your grade school studies in fractions, you will realize just how many different combinations can make up four quarters.

Other commonly used rhythmic devices are *triplets, ties,* and *dots.* Three notes grouped together under the triplet sign are played or sung in the time usually taken by two of them: an eighth-note triplet is executed in the time value of a quarter note, a quarter-note triplet in the time value of a half note, and so on.

A tie literally ties two notes of the same pitch together so that the second one is not rearticulated. Ties are used when a note is to be held over a barline or when you need to use two notes instead of one larger one so as not to obscure the beat.

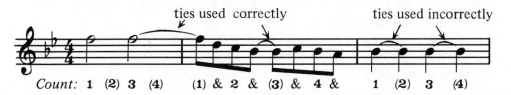

Don't confuse ties with *slurs,* or *phrase marks,* which look the same as ties. These are placed over two or more notes of different pitches to indicate different things to players of different instruments or to tell a singer that one syllable of a song is sung over several pitches.

A dot placed after a note increases that note's value by one-half: a dotted quarter note is equal in time value to a quarter note plus an eighth note, a dotted half note to a half note plus a quarter, and so on.

Since so many popular song forms feature repetition, it is useful to know about the forms of repeat signs and how they are used. These devices are also practical for saving space when writing out your song and for avoiding page turns. Using a repeat sign, whether it's a repeat of one measure or a whole chorus, rather than writing the section out again alerts the reader that he has played this part before; that there is nothing new here to worry about.

The most basic repeat sign is two dots followed by a barline and a heavy line. It tells you to go back to a point in the piece where you see the same sign reversed.

If there is no reversed repeat sign, go back to the beginning (where else?). The second time you encounter the repeat sign, ignore it.

If the last few bars are different the second time through, you can use first and second endings. These tell the reader to play or sing the music under the first bracket the first time through, but to skip these measures on the repeat and use the ones under the second bracket instead.

You can also have third, fourth, and more endings if you need them, or you can have one ending that is used the first and third times and one for the second and fourth times or any similar arrangement.

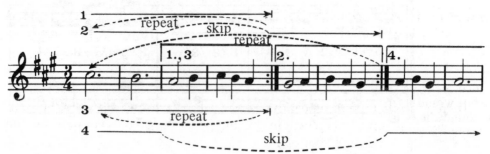

Other useful repeat signs are *D.C.* and *D.S. D.C.* stands for the Italian *da capo* ("from the head") and means to go back to the very beginning and start over. *D.S.* stands for *dal segno* ("from the sign") and sends you back to the point at which you see the sign 𝄋 over the staff. If you want to repeat one section and then skip to a final ending of some sort, use *D.C. al coda* or *D.S. al coda*. These send you back to the beginning or the sign, but you only go until you see the sign ⊕ . At that point you jump to the end of the piece where you see the sign ⊕ repeated and play the final section, or *coda*.

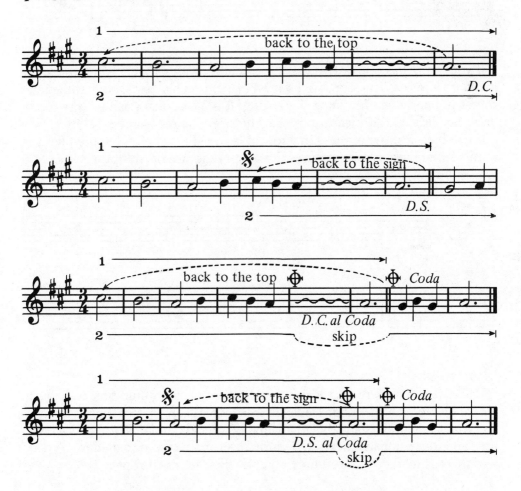

There is also a type of repeat that sends you back to the top, or to the sign, and tells you to end somewhere in the middle, at the point where you see the word *Fine* (pronounced "feenay").

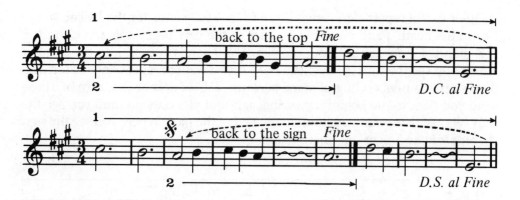

If your song has one or two measures that repeat, you may want to use the *measure repeat sign*. This sign is often used in instrumental parts, but it sometimes comes in handy when writing out a song. It is a diagonal slash with two dots on either side, and it means to repeat the previous measure verbatim.

If you have a string of these in a row, it is sometimes helpful to the player to number them every few measures. It's best not to use one of these symbols at the beginning of a new line.

## Leadsheets

The leadsheet is perhaps the most vital means of communication available to the songwriter. A well-written leadsheet is like a roadmap of your song and makes it immediately understandable to anyone who reads music. This will save you time and frustration in rehearsal, performance, and recording situations. A good leadsheet is made up of certain elements. (See sample on page 107.)

A.    *Title:* Put the complete title at the top center of the first page. There is special manuscript paper that has only eight staves on the first page, leaving a large blank space at the top for the title. It is usually called "leadsheet" paper or "8/10" (subsequent pages have ten staves). If you cannot find this type of manuscript paper, use ten-stave paper and cover the top staff on the first page with white tape to give you space to make the title nice and large.

   If the sheet runs more than one page, put the title or an abbreviation of the title next to the page number on each subsequent page.

B/C.   *Lyricist/Composer:*  The example below shows the traditional placement. However, both names or a single name may appear in position C in one of the following formats:

   Words and music by
   Peter Pickow


   Lyrics by Amy Appleby


   Music by Peter Pickow
   Lyrics by Amy Appleby and Peter Pickow

D.   *Tempo marking:* This should be a concise indication of the intended tempo, and sometimes the style or feel as well, of the song. For instance:
   Slowly and freely
   Not too fast
   Rock ballad
   Medium swing
   Moderate
   Very fast
Note that only the first letter of the first word is capitalized.

E.   *Key signature:* Due to the short nature of popular songs the typical leadsheet is usually under two pages, and many copyists place the key signature only at the beginning. Traditional practice places it at the beginning of each staff. It is a good practice to follow, especially if any of the sections of your song modulate (change key).

F.   *Time signature:* After the key signature comes the time signature. This is placed only at the beginning of the leadsheet, unless the meter changes, at which point the new signature appears.

G.   *Melody line:* Write out the melody neatly and simply. Be sure to plan ahead so that there is room for the melody line to correspond clearly with the lyric. You may want to do a dummy leadsheet first to sketch how the final copy will lay out. As a rule, put two to four measures on a line and maintain approximately equal spacing between barlines. Decide on the simplest form of the melody, and don't worry about strict notation of stylistic embellishments that you add when you sing or play the song.

H.   *Lyric:* Use hyphens to break each word into syllables, and center each syllable or word of the lyric directly beneath the note of the melody it goes with. Notice that a line is used to indicate when the last syllable of a word or a one-syllable word should be held for more than one note.

     If any section has two sets of words, for instance, a first and second verse, put both in. You will sometimes see three sets of words under a repeated section of music. This is okay if you can fit them in neatly. It is best to put anything over two sets of words at the end of the leadsheet under the heading "Additional Lyrics" or "Extra Verses." Many copyists also append a complete typed set of lyrics at the end of the sheet to clarify the order of the sections.

I.   *Chord symbols:* Like the melody line, you'll want to keep the chord symbols neat and simple to outline the basic chord progression of the song. Unless altered chords or inversions are an integral part of the harmony, it is best to reduce a complex progression like Cmaj13 F6/9 G7♭5♭9 to its basic harmony—C F G7. Anyone who is reading your chart wants to get a grasp of the song quickly and easily and complicated chord names can slow down comprehension.

J.   *Section letters:* These are also known as rehearsal letters, because they give songwriters and musicians a way to refer to the sections of a song during rehearsal. You might want to put a section letter at the beginning of each important segment of the song. The first section letter, A, does not go at the very beginning because you can always say, "Take it from the top."

     Sometimes Arabic- or Roman-numeral rehearsal numbers are used. These are less likely than letters to be confused with chord symbols, but they may be confused with measure numbers.

K.   *Measure numbers:* Sometimes measure numbers are used instead of section letters to provide points of reference in the song. If you use measure numbers in your leadsheet, mark the measure number that occurs at the beginning of each staff, or place a number every five measures.

L.   *Section heads:* If your song breaks down conveniently into intro, verse, chorus, and bridge sections, you might want to put these in, too.

M.   *Rhythm figures:* For the most part, the rhythm of your song is conveyed by its melody line. However, the rhythm-figure system of slash marks can be very useful to indicate unusual rhythms, accents, or stops during those parts of the song where the vocal line is absent. As with melody line and chord symbols, don't try to put too much into rhythm figures. Notice how they are used in the example; only to sketch an important rhythmic idea or stop at a point at which there might be confusion.

N. **Copyright notice:** Whether or not you have registered your song for copyright, it is copyrighted by law from the moment you create it. You should always include a copyright notice at the bottom of the first page of music. A valid copyright notice includes the word copyright or the copyright symbol ©, the year, and the writer's name.

*Chord Charts*

Although the standard leadsheet format is good for conveying the big picture, it is not always necessary. Instrumentalists usually find a chord chart of some type to be sufficient, sometimes even preferable. To be useful, a chord chart must clearly show the chords and when they change. The easiest way to do this is to write or type out the complete lyric of the song and place each chord directly above the word or syllable of the change. This system works best for songs that are simple or in situations where the musicians have time to become familiar with the song.

Verse:

        D       F#m7
If it's lovin' you want,

        Em7     A7
Well, you know I'm around,

           D      F#m7
If you just want someone to talk to,

 Em7      A7
I won't make a sound.

 (G)    F#m7   Bm7
If you just want to use me,

    G7     A7
As a shoulder to cry on.

    Em    G    F#7    (stop)
Or a shadow to follow you around,

Chorus:

   Bm7    F#m7
I'm available

    Em7         G
And my intentions are good

F#7 Bm7   F#m7
I'm available

    Em7     G7
And it should be understood

  A7     D   Bm       F#7#9 (stop)
That you're the only one who can see

     Bm   Bb   C
My availability.

Somewhere in between the lyric sheet and the leadsheet lies the true chord chart. This is usually written out using the rhythm-figure notation discussed previously. The slash marks use the same system of open and filled-in "noteheads," and stems, flags, and beams as do normal notes with the one exception that the quarter-note slash mark is usually drawn without a stem. If the rhythm is consistent, it is sufficient to use just quarter-note slashes.

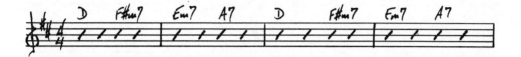

It's easy to expand on this system when the need arises: if there is a riff or musical hook that is important, you can lapse into standard notation to communicate it. If there are stops or pushes (anticipated rhythms) that you want the whole band to do, you can write them in. If chords change off the beat, it's simple to make clear.

What makes this type of chord chart so versatile is that it can be used by any instrumentalist, from a drummer to a rhythm guitarist to a tenor sax soloist. If you put the lyric in, even singers can use it, provided they know the tune.

### Arrangements and Instrumental Parts

Writing out an actual note-for-note arrangement is seldom done with popular songs, with the exception of parts for string or horn sections, backup singers, or other orchestral groups. To create these types of parts requires arranging and music notation know-how, and since it is not truly part of writing a song, we won't go into detail here. Keep in mind that what might sound like great horn or string voicings when figured out on piano or guitar or in your head will not necessarily sound that way when played by the actual instruments. If you do decide to try your hand at this type of arrangement, it is best to get help from an experienced arranger.

## Demo Techniques

If you have any experience with recording, at home or in the studio, solo or with a band, the first thing to realize is that a song demo should be considered very differently from a demo to promote a band or a singer. There are two schools of thought on how a song demo should be produced: the "bare-bones" approach and the "releaseable" approach.

Songwriters following the bare-bones approach hold that the most important aspect is letting the song speak for itself without attaching any preconceived ideas of instrumentation, arrangement, or production. Demos of this type usually consist of one singer singing the song once through with the simplest backup possible (usually a single acoustic guitar or piano). There should be no instrumental breaks, except perhaps a simple introduction or short instrumental interlude.

The idea is to allow the listener to use his imagination. If the listener is a singer, he will be able to hear himself singing this song. If the listener is the A&R (artists and repertoire) man of a record label, he will be able to imagine several of his artists doing this song. For instance, would you think that Erroll Garner's jazz standard "Misty" could be a Top 40 hit for artists as disparate as pop singer Johnny Mathis, R&B great Lloyd Price, and country comedian Ray Stevens? If you had heard one of these artists' recordings while looking for material for one of the others, would you have picked this song?

While the bare-bones approach is still a good one for today's songwriter, if you are performing original material, you may want to go toward the other extreme, the "releaseable" approach. The song demo should sound as close to a finished product as possible. This involves a high quality of musicianship as well as state-of-the-art production values. It is a gamble that has paid off for many new artists, but has sent many more to the poorhouse.

Somewhere in between these two approaches lies the idea of trying to make your song demo sound as if it had been done by the artist you would like to see record it. This is never a good idea. A perfect imitation is likely to unnerve most artists, an imperfect one will sound like a parody. Either way, the attempt is not likely to be appreciated.

### Home Recording Tips

These days, almost anyone who wants to can afford to set up a decent amateur home recording studio. If you are serious about music, you probably have a good stereo system, and if you are an instrumentalist as well you probably have some other audio-related equipment lying around too. To get started making a home demo, all you need is a quiet space, a good cassette or reel-to-reel tape deck with a microphone, and whatever instruments you want to use (along with whomever you need to play them). Even if you are performing your song solo and using this basic recording setup, have someone else around to act as producer and recording engineer who will listen to your performance with a critical ear, give you some honest feedback on how it sounds, and take care of the technical end (starting and stopping the tape recorder, for instance).

If you want to get a bit more involved in home recording, you may want to invest in a four-track cassette deck. In recent years, manufacturers have been offering these machines at ever-decreasing prices. These machines allow you to perform some aspects of basic "studio magic" like *overdubbing, punching in,* and *mixing.*

Through overdubbing, you can record one part of your arrangement, say, a rhythm guitar part, all the way through, and then listen to the playback of this track while recording another part, say, your lead vocal, on another track. When you play back the two tracks together, they sound as if they had been done at the same time. The advantages of this technique are many: if you make a mistake in the overdubbed track, you can do it over without having to redo any other tracks.

By punching in, you can even redo only part of a performance. Say that you had recorded a rhythm guitar part on track 1. You then played that track back as you recorded your vocal on track 2. When you listened to them together, everything was fine except that during the last chorus your voice cracked. Punching in on track 2 allows you to start rerecording the vocal in the middle of the song, so you can keep the good part and only have to redo the unsatisfactory section at the end. Another advantage of overdubbing is that it allows you to audition different takes of the same material. Taking the same example, let's assume that the vocal was not all that bad and you thought that you could do it better but weren't sure. What you can do at this point is to move on to track

3 and record a new vocal track from the beginning. Since you are keeping the vocal on track 2, you can listen to both *takes* and choose the best one.

A four-track machine also gives you the benefit of being able to mix the recorded tracks. Even in the simplest situations, this can be a blessing. If you record yourself singing and playing an instrument live (that is, at the same time with no over-dubs), what goes on the tape is what you are stuck with. Upon listening back to it, if the instrument is drowning out your voice at times, you have no choice but to redo the entire song. If you have used overdubbing techniques, you have individual control over each track, allowing you to bring the instrumental track to the foreground at times, and then bring it back down as necessary. This means that you need a separate *mixdown* tape deck to record your final mix.

## MIDI

*MIDI* is an acronym for Musical Instrument Digital Interface. It is a software-based computer language that was originally developed to allow one synthesizer to control another. However, the developers of the language were sufficiently far-sighted to make it flexible enough to allow for many other uses and applications. Today there are hundreds of types of computer software programs and stand-alone devices that make use of MIDI to allow for much more than its original "master/slave" implementation.

For songwriters, the most obvious applications are the many computer programs tailored for music composition and notation. These allow you to play a tune on a MIDI-equipped keyboard, record the information digitally on a home computer, display, manipulate, and save this information on the computer screen, and then play it back through any number of MIDI-equipped synthesizers and drum machines. Some programs will even translate the music you play into standard music notation, allow you to add lyrics, and print out a finished leadsheet. Others provide the equivalent of a multitrack recording facility, so that you can lay down as many as sixty-four separate instrumental tracks. (It is rumored that one of Sting's hobbies is inputting and playing back entire Mahler symphonies.) The features of the various programs and systems are so varied, and are changing so rapidly, that it would be out of place to attempt even a survey here.

## Synthesizers, Sequencers, and Drum Machines

Aside from the MIDI/computer connection, synthesizers, sequencers, and drum machines may serve as functional songwriting aids. Sequencers are actually small dedicated computers that can record what is played on a synthesizer and replay it verbatim. Most do not offer much control over changing what has been recorded, other than changing tempo or rearranging and linking different sections. However, the ability to perform these operations can make all the difference if you are not an accomplished instrumentalist. For instance, you can record a simple keyboard part at a slow tempo, and then speed up the playback. Or you can record the verse and chorus sections just once, and then repeat and rearrange them in any order to try out different formats for the song.

With so much popular music being rhythmically oriented, a good drum machine can be a real boon. It is a simple matter to program and arrange rhythmic patterns into an outline for a song on these devices. Many contemporary songwriters use this method of starting from a rhythmic model, especially those writing dance music.

### Studio Recording Tips

Going into a professional recording studio to make a song demo requires commitment, but with a moderate amount of planning ahead and a realistic, professional attitude, taking this path can provide very satisfying and cost-effective results. First of all, decide on what you want to end up with. If you go looking for a studio without a clear idea of what you intend to accomplish, you will not get very far in evaluating your choices. Determine such factors as how many songs you need to record, what the instrumentation will be for each song, and whether the session can be done live or if you will need to overdub. If you are using other musicians on your recording, make sure you know how comfortable they are with the material and with the recording process.

Next, look for a studio in your area. The best way to find a studio is to ask fellow musicians or songwriters for their recommendations. Musicians of all levels of experience are likely to have done local studio work, usually working on song or band demos. What they can tell you about their experiences will give you a good idea of what is out there. If you don't know anyone who is up on the local music scene, try looking for advertisements in a local music paper or in the music section of the classifieds in your local newspaper.

After you have determined your options, make appointments to visit the facilities. Most owners of small studios are proud of their establishments and will be only too happy to show you around and discuss your needs. This is where your planning begins to come in handy. In talking with the studio owner, be clear about what you want to do and how you want to do it. Ask him what he would recommend for this type of session. If you want to do a simple song demo of just you singing and accompanying yourself on piano, beware of a studio that places a lot of emphasis on their multitrack capabilities, outboard signal processing equipment, and computerized mixdown facility.

If you find a studio you like, and where you like the people that work there, you can start to discuss price. This is another point at which good planning pays off. Some studios have different prices for different times of day; some will discount their basic hourly rate if you book time a certain period in advance, or if you book a certain amount of consecutive time. In addition, there are different rates depending on what studio equipment you will be using; a simple direct-to-two-track live recording, for example, should cost less per hour than an eight- or sixteen-track session. When figuring how much time you will need, be sure to include time for mixing and editing. If you have given the studio owner or engineer a good idea of what your project entails, he should be able to help you estimate this.

With all these questions settled, be sure to book the studio time far enough in advance to give you a chance to rehearse and plan the session. Nothing runs up the clock in the studio like rehearsing. No matter who is paying for it, everyone feels bad when things don't come together. If you are going it alone, make sure you know your material backward and forward. If you have other musicians or singers on the session, rehearse them ahead of time to the point where there will be no surprises. Either way, have a firm program of what you are going to do and stick to that order. This type of rehearsing and planning will also ensure that you do not try to do too much in one session. If you are doing several songs, it may be better to plan two or more short sessions rather than one marathon.

### Getting Your Ideas Across to Musicians and Engineers

There is an art to communicating with musicians and recording engineers. This talent is evident in any really good producer, and unless you are lucky enough to know someone with production experience, you will be producing your own song demo, whether at home or in the studio. The way to excel at this kind of communication is to listen. This may be difficult if you are also performing on the session, but, nevertheless, listen to everyone. Listen to what they say and listen to what they play. At every point in the process, try to distance yourself and listen as if you are hearing it for the first time.

While you are listening to everyone else, do not forget that you are in charge. Don't be afraid to tell a guitar player that his part is too busy, or the engineer that there is not enough reverb on the vocal. Your song demo is your expression of what you believe your song to be: you have to be able to make it your own.

# 9

# *Blues*

*A lot of people think blues singers write when they're sad and lonely. They think you gotta be down and out to write the blues—hungry, broke. It's not true. I write when I've got a good feeling, when I'm happy. When things are going well for you, you write. You have to be in the groove to write. You can't be upset and worried about the blues.*

—*John Lee Hooker*

## A Brief History

The blues began in the American South. Its earliest roots lie in the field-hollers and work songs that were chanted and sung by slaves in pre–Civil War times. Although these repetitive and rhythmic chants helped pace and coordinate the movements of the workers in the field, they also provided one of the few forms of group expression permissible to Afro-American people of this period. As such, these songs had a deep unifying power for the American black and echoed elements of the vital African sense of sound and rhythm. Sometimes the seemingly innocent words of work songs had concealed references to the black slave's dream of freedom and contempt for the white owner.

In the troubled years following the abolition of slavery, blacks continued to express feelings of misery and desperation through music. Though "free," many suffered the same deprivation they had endured as slaves, yet now the song themes were not exclusively work-related. Political, economic, and personal issues could be freely addressed in song, and the songs of this period of black history form the basis of the traditional country blues.

### The Blues Comes to Town

W. C. Handy is considered the father of the blues, for he recognized the universal appeal of the growing Afro-American musical tradition and composed the first blues songs to be commercially accepted. In 1912 Handy brought the blues out of its rural home to the urban center of the popular music of the day, Tin Pan Alley, when he became the first songwriter to have a blues song published— "The Memphis Blues." The form was readily accepted by the listening public and many more blues songs followed. Handy's "St. Louis Blues" of 1914 and Jelly Roll Morton's "Jelly Roll Blues" of 1915 were two of the most successful blues songs of this period. American popular music was changing rapidly in this early portion of the century, largely due to the influences of Afro-American musical traditions. The public immediately recognized the greatness of this "new" music and accepted the black songwriter and performer as a welcome relief from the staid Victorian songs that had been popular before. Ragtime music, the forerunner of jazz, was already the rage of Tin Pan Alley, and the black spiritual was giving way to the gospel music we know today. The blues was in very good company.

### Blues on the Delta

The Mississippi Delta region was the heartland of the American blues. This area produced many of the great blues writers and musicians and served as the hub of the country blues during its heyday from 1915 to 1940. Here, legendary itinerant bluesmen like Robert Johnson and Charley Patton perfected their craft and influenced scores of other songwriters and musicians throughout the region. By 1930, the standard blues forms had developed and solidified, and the voice of the blues was beginning to reach the urban centers of the United States, particularly the cities of the industrial North.

### Chicago Blues

The booming post–World War II economy caused many black southerners to migrate to the northern industrial cities in search of new jobs and a more tolerant atmosphere. Cleveland, Detroit, and particularly Chicago became new homes for the blues. Rural blacks moving to these cities carried with them the rich musical heritage of the South. In this new setting, the old music served a dual purpose. It provided a reminder of home and the way of life that they had left behind, and it was a way to express their reactions to the urban environment. Artists and songwriters like T-Bone Walker, B. B. King, and Muddy Waters experimented with more sophisticated blues chord progressions and song forms, and expanded and electrified the traditional blues instrumentation. The Chicago Blues had arrived. Songs like B. B. King's "The Thrill Is Gone" and T-Bone Walker's "Stormy Monday" brought a new intensity to the blues sound and a resurgence of listeners across the country.

## So-Called Blues

Ever since the blues came to Tin Pan Alley, there have been successful songs whose titles claim them as "blues" songs; yet they actually have very little in common with the established forms. These include songs like "Lovesick Blues," (originally written by Cliff Friend as a novelty vaudeville number and later rewritten by Hank Williams as an up-tempo country lament), "Basin Street Blues," and "Folsom Prison Blues." These "so-called blues" songs use the term to invoke a general state of mind, "having the blues," rather than implying a specific musical style or form.

## The Many Faces of the Blues

In addition to fostering a direct descendent, rhythm and blues, the blues has influenced every other style of American popular music. In turn, different genres have developed blues styles of their own. These hybrid styles all use the characteristic blues scale and harmonization and often incorporate blues themes in the lyric as well.

Since rock and roll is really the child of blues and country music, it's no surprise that rock has its own form of the blues. Blues-rock songs such as Cream's versions of "Spoonful" and "Crossroads" are simply revivals or adaptations of traditional blues songs. Others are modern originals, like "Ain't No Sunshine" and "Stormy Monday." Basically, blues-rock songs are blues songs played with a rock beat by a rock band. The success of such artists as Paul Butterfield, George Thorogood, and Eric Clapton is a testament to the popularity of this idiom.

The term "country blues" is often used to designate all traditional rural blues forms. However, what we are talking about here is the strong influence of the blues in country music. In fact, Jimmie Rodgers (1898–1933), "the Father of Country Music," was considered something of a blues singer/songwriter by his contemporaries. Some of his early "blue yodels," "T for Texas," for instance, are traditional blues songs in format and subject matter. In later years he wrote several of country music's own brand of "so-called" blues—"Blues for Dixie," "Gambling Polka-Dot Blues," "Miss the Mississippi"—many of which are performed today. Listen to the songs of great country songwriters like Hank Williams, Willie Nelson, and Merle Haggard to hear more examples of the pervasive influence of the blues in country music. You will also hear echoes of the blues in the bluegrass branch of country music. Bill Monroe, the originator and foremost proponent of bluegrass, cites the blues as being a primary influence in the development of this style.

Songs like "Good Morning Heartache" and "Basin Street Blues" show a strong jazz influence, a natural combination of related styles. Blues separated itself distinctly from jazz with the advent of rhythm and blues in the 1940s. For a discussion of this later blues style, refer to the chapter on "The Black Sound."

Traditional blues is still alive and well in the music of such artists as George Thorogood and B. B. King. Very recently, there has been a resurgence of interest in writing new, pure blues songs. Perhaps as a reaction to the prepackaged synthesizer sound of today, songwriters and performers have again turned to the blues in an effort to recapture a more personal and emotional voice. Remember that the blues helped to shape and still influences every other type of music popular today, from country to rock and roll. For this reason, it is well worth studying the blues. You will be able to apply its essence to whatever kind of songs you like to write.

## Blues Themes

The earliest blues were about the tough side of living. Themes like homelessness, poverty, alcoholism, drug addiction, and broken relationships were addressed in plain terms, with unguarded emotion. Classics like "Sometimes I Feel Like a Motherless Child," "Empty Pocket Blues," "Alcoholic Blues," and "Baby, Please Don't Go" openly addressed issues that other forms of popular song dealt with only obliquely. Today, blues themes still center around the down side of life and, even by today's liberal standards, are often quite controversial. The important thing to realize about blues songs is that, at root, they are all about "having the blues" for one reason or another.

The raw, personal tone of the blues performance and the confessional nature of blues themes provide a good platform for the expression of human drama and pain. Because a good blues song calls for stark sincerity on the part of the songwriter and performer, be sure the themes you choose have the ring of truth. The only way to make this happen is to write straight from the heart.

## The Blues Title

Many classic blues songs are identified as blues in their titles: "Yellow Dog Blues," "The Railroad Blues." Many also indicate the area of their origin, or the setting for their action: "Louisiana Blues," "Mississippi Blues," "St. Louis Blues." Others use the term to mean the "blue mood," more than the style of music itself: "Good Morning Blues," "Crazy Blues," "Trouble Blues." Some titles even explain the reason for the singer's sorrow: "Empty Bed Blues," "Bad Luck Blues," "Lonesome Road Blues."

A blues title need not contain the word "blues" to be effective. Some blues titles depict difficult personal situations: "My First Wife Left Me," and "Back Door Man." Others speak of social problems and loneliness: "Walked All Night Long," "Ball and Chain," "Rolling Stone." This kind of title should create a situation or image of human trouble from one person's point of view. Remember, the story of the blues is the story of human sorrow and struggle, told in the first person.

## The Blues Lyric

Like the title, a blues song's lyric should reflect a first-person or narrative voice and express frustration, longing, or lament in conversational language about a problem or theme of importance to everyone. Since the message of the blues is so direct and simple, its language is limited. Words must be kept to a minimum, and statements are straightforward and unadorned. This creates a powerful effect in light of the characteristic repetition of the basic twelve-bar blues verse form, a rhyming couplet with the first line repeated. This three-line verse is the classic form of the blues lyric.

> *Woke up this morning, blues all 'round my bed,*
> *Well, I woke up this morning, and the blues was all around my bed,*
> *Went down to the kitchen, blues was even in my bread.*

Other verse forms use different arrangements of repeated and rhyming lines.

> *Goin' down that road feelin' bad,*
> *Oh, I'm goin' down that road feelin' bad,*
> *Yes, I'm goin' down that road feelin' bad, Lord, Lord,*
> *And I ain't goin' to be treated this-a-way.*

Although there are many variations on the blues verse form, in most songs the first line of the lyric is repeated at least once. However, there are some notable exceptions to this pattern.

> *You're gonna quit me, baby,*
> *Good as I've been to you,*
> *Good as I've been to you, Lord, Lord,*
> *Good as I've been to you.*

### The Vocabulary of the Blues

Since the blues started in the American South, the lyrics contain many of the colloquialisms and rhythms of black southern speech. Blues lyrics often contain dialect spellings of words or colloquial phrases.

> *He was a travelin' man,*
> *Certainly was a travelin' man,*
> *He was the most travelinest man,*
> *That ever was in this land.*

As the blues moved to the urban North, blues lyrics retained some of the dialect and phrasings of the black South as did the everyday speech of blacks in their new city environment.

> *Chicago's tough, Chicago's mean,*
> *Chicago's tough, Chicago's mean,*
> *Worst ol' city I ever done seen.*

Notice how each of these blues lyrics center on one strong theme and use simple and natural language, rather than clever turns of phrase, to get across their messages. When writing your own blues lyrics, try to avoid using words with a lot of syllables, or words that are not common to ordinary conversation. Also remember, the predictable use of repetition in the lyric lends that familiar blues feeling to a song. So, the trick to writing good blues lyrics is to stay within the boundaries of the simple forms and still say something fresh and powerful.

### Imagery

Because the writers of the blues were often country people in a rural environment, natural imagery and symbolism was a focal point for many great blues songs. Traditional images include fields, valleys, the sun and moon, river banks, mountains, and country roads. Traveling was a way of life for the early bluesmen and the many itinerant homeless of the black lower class. The roadside and natural images provide a compelling sense of action and direction in many blues lyrics. Sometimes images from nature had implied or symbolic meaning. For instance, the image of a river traditionally suggests death or even spiritual rebirth.

Images from the life of field workers and prisoners also appear often in blues lyrics. Trains, campfires, and makeshift luggage are frequent blues images that symbolize the life of the hobo or traveling blues musician.

Urban blues lyrics often incorporate the imagery of the barroom, tenement, whorehouse, worksite, and factory to illustrate the difficulties of city life. Sometimes the lyric centers on the problems of adapting to city life itself.

> *I'm just from the country,*
> *Never been to your town before,*
> *Lord, I'm broke and hungry,*
> *Ain't got no place to go.*

Broken relationships and sexual encounters provide the imagery for many powerful blues songs. This kind of imagery is favored particularly by blues songwriters of today, because it deals with a theme more relevant to the lives of today's blues listeners.

> *Baby, please don't go,*
> *Baby, please don't go,*
> *Baby, please don't go way down to New Orleans,*
> *You know I love you so.*

A blues verse should contain only one or two prominent images to illustrate the singer's predicament or state of mind. The blues verse forms are fragmentary and do not lend themselves to narrative, but be sure that the images in all the song's verses work together to paint a unified picture of one person's view of a difficult situation.

### Blues Rhyme

The blues allows for a lot of freedom when it comes to creating rhyme. In the previous examples, you will see quite a few imperfect rhymes like "long" and "gone" or "before" and "go." Though loose rhymes like these would not be appropriate in other musical styles, they are a mainstay of the blues lyric. It is almost as if the speaker is so blue, he doesn't have time for perfect rhyme. The pure message of the blues is more important.

Notice that many of the imperfect rhymes in blues songs only sound natural when sung with a southern accent. Since almost every commercial blues song is performed with a southern dialect or black urban lilt, it's good to create rhymes that sound natural in this vein. Even a white performer like James Taylor gets a country tone in his voice when singing the blues. This isn't a phony tactic if executed with discretion; it's a performer's concession to the demands of a particular musical style.

## The Music of the Blues

Certain factors qualify a song as true blues and if you are looking for an authentic sound, then you should stick to these basic guidelines. Writing songs that adhere to a strict blues form is a good way to develop your ear for the bluesy elements you may want to inject in other songwriting styles.

### The Blues Melody

The melody of the song should be built from the traditional blues scale or from a major scale with the characteristically flatted blue notes. These notes, especially the flatted third, create the idiomatic modal ambiguity of the blues melody, somewhere in between major and minor.

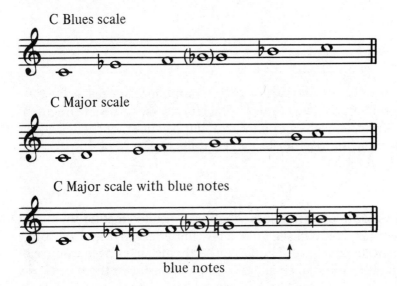

The flatted fifth, shown in parentheses above, is a modern innovation and is not seen in older blues melodies.

Try playing or singing these few blues clichés. As you do, identify the blue notes, where they are placed, and how they resolve.

## Harmony

Remember that the blues vocalist often bends notes to produce *quarter tones* (pitches in between the notes in the scale), so the harmony should be quite straightforward and not conflict with these nuances in the performance of the melody. The most common format for verses is the *twelve-bar blues* format. This name comes from the number of measures in the repeating chord progression. The twelve-bar blues format is not only used in blues songs but is the basis for countless songs in every genre, especially in rock. Here is the basic twelve-bar blues progression in the key of E. Notice that all chords are Dominant Sevenths.

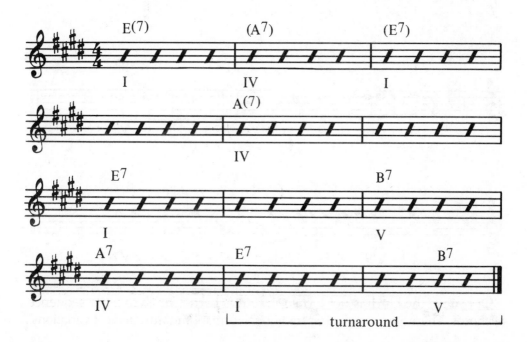

An interesting characteristic of this form is the turnaround section in the last two bars. The turnaround in the example above is a simple variant but clearly shows the function of this section: to cause the progression to end on the V7 chord, which then sends you back to the beginning. Although the melody and lyric are usually out before the turnaround begins, this is the place to work some individuality into your blues song. Here are a few standard blues turnarounds. (The last of these is similar to the one James Taylor used as a signature riff in "Steamroller Blues.") Try coming up with some variations of your own.

Of course, the blues is not locked in to this particular twelve-bar sequence of chords. There are several other traditional formats and hundreds of variations.

## Rhythm

The meter of the song should be simple and strong—usually in $\frac{4}{4}$ time. Slow blues with a backbeat may be written, or felt, in $\frac{6}{4}$ time with an accent on the four of each measure and a lesser accent on one.

The rhythm is usually of the *shuffle* variety, in which each group of two eighth notes is felt in a triplet rhythm.

To express this rhythm more precisely, blues songs are often written out in $\frac{12}{8}$ time.

The tempos of blues songs range from moderate, driving uptunes to slow ballads, but the blues ballad is the most common.

The key to writing successful blues is to keep it simple. Don't be afraid to rein-force musical and lyric ideas with repetition. The traditional blues sound can be a real pleasure to capture in your own material. Don't apply your creative powers to reinventing the basic blues patterns and structure; it simply can't be done. You'll make the best use of your energies by coming up with a fresh and meaningful blues interpretation that stays within the rules.

# 10

# *Jazz*

*In the past decades jazz has acquired both polish and a good deal more variety, and it has taken on different forms such as bop, progressive jazz, "modern," "intellectual," "cerebral," even a revival of Dixieland. Whatever your reaction to such refinements, improvisation is the basis on which good jazz rests.*

*—Benny Goodman*

*The funeral marches are played on the way to the cemetery. And I learned such songs as "When the Saints Go Marching In," "High Society," "Oh, Didn't He Ramble?" and others. But a large part of the music was on the spur of the moment, made up and played by ear. There was the tail-gate trombone—who sat on the tail-gate of the wagon carrying the band—those who marched, played, and sang. There were the rented Cadillacs, the nurses who attended the relatives, and all the others who came to mourn his passing and rejoice in his resurrection. But the real music began around the grave. That was how jazz began. That's why it brings people to life.*

*—Louis Armstrong*

## A Brief History

There are many theories as to the origins of jazz, and its true beginnings will probably never be known for sure. Around 1900, jazz emerged as a distinct musical form, distinguished from blues and ragtime. All three of these musical styles are an outgrowth of the rich black American folk tradition of the nineteenth century, but both jazz and ragtime bear the mark of many other European and American influences. Jazz took some of its form and rhythm from American dance and folk music, particularly that influenced by dance music of Spain, Britain, and the gypsy cultures of Europe. Traditional fiddle music also played a role in helping to shape early jazz. Coming from such a broad spectrum of musical styles, it is no wonder that jazz ultimately claimed the worldwide acceptance it has today.

### New Orleans—Birthplace of Jazz

By the turn of the century, some black folk music of the American South used the syncopated rhythms that characterize jazz music. While jazz pioneer Jelly Roll Morton's famous quote, "Jazz started in New Orleans," is probably a bit oversimplified, that city is certainly where jazz came of age. Although it didn't yet have a name, the new music flourished in the saloons, dance halls, and brothels of the thriving seaport. At this point, jazz was basically instrumental dance music, and jazz ensembles featured such instruments as cornet, trombone, clarinet, piano, guitar, banjo, tuba, bass-saxophone, and drums. The early Dixieland jazz of New Orleans was distinguished from other forms of popular music because it featured instrumental solos, improvisation in performance, and the new jazz beat, characterized by flexible rhythms and syncopation. The melodic, harmonic, and rhythmic conventions that grew out of these early musicians' improvisations laid the foundation of jazz as we know it today.

### Jazz Moves Upriver

By 1917, jazz had moved northward and St. Louis and Kansas City had become centers for jazz activity. Jazz bands were growing rapidly in size and number and, by the mid-twenties, written band arrangements began to appear. Though many jazzmen continued their work in the cities of the industrial North, St. Louis, Kansas City, and, of course, New Orleans have remained jazz centers of the world until this day.

### Chicago and New York

At the same time that jazz was becoming popular in the South and Midwest, numerous clubs in Harlem and Chicago were featuring the jazz sound. Jazz musicians were drawn to these northern cities both by the prospect of performance work and by the newly born recording industry that was now surging, particularly in Chicago. In fact, the birth of jazz coincided very neatly with the birth of the recording industry, which is what made it possible for jazz to become an international craze by the mid-twenties.

Many of the early jazz recordings we hear today were made in Chicago. There, jazz greats like Jelly Roll Morton, King Oliver, and Louis Armstrong did their early work, and it was there that white musicians like Eddie Condon and Bud Freeman started making their contribution to the growing jazz movement. The typical Chicago jazz band incorporated the saxophone and, as a result, jazz began to move toward the "cooler" sound characteristic of the 1940s.

In Harlem, several large black theaters opened in the teens and twenties and provided a venue for the black jazz musician. The twenties and thirties saw the heyday of jazz in New York at legendary clubs like Count Basie's and the Cotton Club. Harlem jazz was characterized by an insistent swing rhythm and the stride piano style, as perfected by early jazz greats like James P. Johnson and Fats Waller.

Both Chicago and New York provided fertile ground for the booming commercial success of jazz, and the jazz of these cities laid the groundwork for the big band swing of the late thirties and forties, and the bebop to come.

### Jazz, Tin Pan Alley, and Broadway

Jazz was largely an instrumental style in its early years and reinterpreted folk tunes formed its original repertoire. Familiar folk songs like "When the Saints Go Marching In," "Frankie and Johnnie," "St. James Infirmary," and "Muskrat Ramble" were typical of the earliest jazz performances. Although many of these were songs, they were rarely sung; or if they were, the vocal was brief and of secondary importance. Since almost any tune could be "jazzed up," at first there was no pressing need for new songs.

As the popularity of jazz grew, reaching a crescendo in the mid-twenties, writers of musical theater and the ever-opportunistic songsmiths of Tin Pan Alley noted its success and began to capitalize on the new craze. Popular songs began to show a marked jazz influence in both music and lyrics: "My Honey's Lovin' Arms" (Joseph Meyer, 1922), "Sweet Georgia Brown" (Ben Bernie, 1925), "If I Could Be with You" (Henry Creamer and James P. Johnson, 1926), "Crazy Rhythm" (Joseph Meyer and Roger Wolfe Kahn, 1928). Jazz musicians continued to adapt songs from the musical theater and other popular styles to add to their repertoire. If a song got played enough, it became known as a jazz *standard*.

## The Jazz Song

Continuing the trend of the twenties, new songs in the jazz idiom continued to be written throughout the thirties and forties. This period saw the rise of the jazz big band, typified by the groups led by Benny Goodman, Artie Shaw, and Glenn Miller, and the arrival of the Swing Era. Although many big band songs became popular or remain familiar only in their instrumental versions, artists like Fats Waller, Cab Calloway, Louis Armstrong, Joe Williams, Lena Horne, Ella Fitzgerald, and Billie Holiday popularized the art of jazz singing.

Jazz also claimed many popular songs, show tunes, and even blues songs for its own, and many of these appropriated songs are now only remembered for their jazz versions. Songs like "Tea for Two," "Button up Your Overcoat," "Love Me or Leave Me," "A Tisket A Tasket," and the songs of jazz-influenced writers like Irving Berlin, George Gershwin, and Jerome Kern were reinterpreted by jazz performers to become jazz songs.

*The Jazz Song Today*

Instrumental jazz continued to develop toward the modern and avant-garde styles familiar today, with the help of progressive jazz artists like Thelonious Monk and Charles Mingus. Though jazz is thought of as a largely instrumental music, the jazz song, as perfected in the thirties and forties, is still very much alive. Artists like Sarah Vaughan, Mel Torme, Bobby Short, Al Jarreau, Bobby McFerrin, and vocal groups like Manhattan Transfer and Singers Unlimited are singing the jazz songs of yesterday and today.

Even pop singers like Joni Mitchell, Linda Ronstadt, and Tom Waits feature jazz and jazz-tinged material. Linda Ronstadt's jazz-pop albums with Nelson Riddle feature standards of the Swing Era, with such numbers as "You Took Advantage of Me" and "But Not for Me." Country star Willie Nelson used jazz standards on several popular albums with jazz-influenced versions of "Blue Skies" and "I'm Gonna Sit Right Down and Write Myself a Letter." Esther Phillips put a great old standard back on the pop charts in 1975 with a surprisingly jazzy version of "What a Difference a Day Makes," which had also been a Top 40 hit for Dinah Washington in 1959. Tom Waits incorporates a more bluesy jazz sound into his performance styles as typified by songs like "The Piano's Been Drinking" and "Small Change Got Rained on with His Own .38." Joni Mitchell uses an almost pure jazz feeling for her version of "Twisted" and "Chair in the Sky," which she wrote with jazz great Charles Mingus. Thus the pop idiom provides a commercial avenue for the jazz song today and today's pop artists and songwriters are well aware of the power of jazz influences in their music.

## Jazz Themes

The early jazz music of writers like Fats Waller and Hoagy Carmichael, and the jazz-swing of Ellington, Count Basie, and Benny Goodman often featured songs with lyrics. The themes of these songs frequently centered on the power of jazz music itself—its sophisticated harmonies, hot melodies, and suggestive rhythms. Walter Donaldson's "Changes" (1927) combines a very inventive progression with a lyric about a jazz musician who loves to play unexpected chords and for this particular talent he's "the talk of Dixieland." Sometimes the creative power of the jazz musician or band was the subject of a song. Many times the lyric was written from the point of view of an avid jazz listener or dancer experiencing a performance and its intoxicating effects.

By the mid-twenties, the music had acquired a glamorous urban mystique and the fast-moving and sophisticated nightlife of jazz musicians and the jazz club set was of great interest to the public at large. Many jazz songs portrayed the reckless and exciting night-on-the-town aspect of the jazz life-style, and this attracted people who came to associate the music with intrigue, romance, and just plain fun. This mixed air of sophistication and earthiness is still the essence of jazz themes today.

## The Jazz Title

Jazz themes often relate to the music itself or to aspects of jazz culture, and this is apparent in many song titles. The legendary jazz clubs provided the theme for many jazz songs of the day. The Savoy Ballroom was commemorated in 1934 with Chick Webb's recording of "Stompin' at the Savoy" and "Savoy Stampede," another tribute, was recorded by Benny Carter. George Shearing's "Lullaby of Birdland" and Joe Zawinul's "Birdland" commemorate another legendary club.

The jazz musician and jazz music itself are often celebrated in song titles. Since improvisation was so much a part of the jazz performance, song themes naturally centered on the excitement of the jazz instrumental, as in "Slap That Bass" and "The Boogie-Woogie Bugle Boy." Jazz titles also extol the virtues of jazz rhythm and feel: "It Don't Mean a Thing if It Ain't Got That Swing," and "Fascinating Rhythm." "Changes" commemorates the excitement of jazz harmony. Titles often reflect the fact that jazz grew out of the blues, as in "Serenade in Blue," "Blue Champagne," and "Mood Indigo."

In the words of W. C. Handy, "Jazz grew up around the fox trot and is still mainly supported by it." Because of this close affinity, many songs glorify jazz-influenced novelty dances. These include the shimmy, the foxtrot and its variants, the Lindy, the quickstep, and various "walks" that imitated the movements of animals like the camel walk and walkin' the dog. Songs like Spencer Williams's "Shim-Me-Sha-Wabble" of 1917 and "Ballin' the Jack," introduced in 1913 by Chris Smith and Jim Burris, initiated various dance crazes in the early jazz years. Dance tunes of the Swing Era include "The Lambeth Walk," Cab Calloway's "The Jumpin' Jive," and Fred Astaire's hit "The Continental." And of course, romance is always a favorite theme, as in "Satin Doll," " 'S Wonderful," "Body and Soul," and "Stardust."

## Jazz Lyrics

In the words of Louis Armstrong, "The basis of jazz is a kind of language. You use it to say all kinds of things and explain all kinds of moods." Since the musical elements are so expressive of mood and image, it's important that you write lyrics that move effortlessly along with the sometimes intricate jazz melody. Jazz uptunes often feature long phrases of melody that never seem to rest. To accommodate this kind of free-flowing melody, many lyrics contain a lot of detail. The first lines of "Lullaby of Birdland" illustrate this kind of fun-loving wordiness.

> *Lullaby of Birdland, that's what I*
> *Always hear when you sigh.*
> *Never in my wordland could there be ways to reveal*
> *In a phrase how I feel.*

Notice how the light-hearted message and irregular phrasing help accommodate the restless and continuous quality of the music.

Jazz lyricists often use nonsense syllables to help point up a melody, as in "Ja-Da:" "Ja Da, Ja Da, Da Ja Da Jing, Jing, Jing." It doesn't mean a lot on its own, but it's sure catchy when you hear it in the context of the song.

When it comes to ballads, jazz lyrics often center on romance. Here, the lyric may also serve an expanded or intricate melody, as in "Stardust," by Hoagy Carmichael and Mitchell Parish.

> *Sometimes I wonder why I spend the lonely night*
> *Dreaming of a song.*

More often, though, the melody phrases of a ballad are much shorter, as in the opening lines of John Green's "Body and Soul."

> *My heart is sad and lonely,*
> *For you I sigh, for you dear only,*

An even simpler lyric is found in the chorus of Duke Ellington's "Mood Indigo."

> *You ain't been blue,*
> *No, no, no.*
> *You ain't been blue,*
> *Till you've had that Mood Indigo.*

As a general rule, if the melody lines are extended and intricate, extend the lyric with full sweeping statements or interesting details. If you intend the lyric for a simpler jazz or jazz-blues melody with shorter phrases, then keep it trim and straightforward.

### The Vocabulary of Jazz

Since many early jazz musicians came from the South, a certain amount of the dialect of that area has remained in jazz lyrics. Colloquialisms and phrasings of the South and of black urban speech are sprinkled throughout many lyrics. Although the language of jazz is often elegant and complex, it can benefit from earthy or casual phrasing, as in "Ain't Misbehavin' " or "It Don't Mean a Thing if It Ain't Got That Swing." It's important that you feel comfortable creating these colloquialisms in your own jazz lyrics. Whatever you do, don't force it, or your lyric will come out sounding insincere. Just find a way of saying what you mean that sounds conversational and fairly impromptu.

### Jazz Imagery

Since jazz started in the South, early writers incorporated the earthy images of southern places and life-styles into their song lyrics. Songs like "Alabamy Bound," "Do You Know What It Means to Miss New Orleans?" and "Georgia on My Mind" perpetuated the southern mystique for the early jazz listener. Favorite images from the southern landscape included rivers, stars, roads, railroads, and assorted flora and fauna—from magnolia trees to possums. Others came from daily life in Dixie, from working in the fields to the strains of a banjo echoing across a river. Many such images of southern life are warmly portrayed in songs like "Washboard Blues," "That's What I Like About the South," "Is It True What They Say About Dixie?" and "When It's Sleepy-Time Down South."

As jazz moved to cities in the North and began to be heard on the Broadway stage and in the movies, jazz lyrics came to include imagery of jazz culture in its sophisticated urban setting. Now city sunsets, trains and taxis, penthouse apartments, flower shops, and the lights on Broadway provided new images for the jazz writer. Jazz clubs, ritzy parties, and cabarets inspired such title images as "Puttin' on the Ritz," "Take the A-Train," "Smoke Rings," and "Blue Champagne." Sometimes the excesses of urban nightlife are suggested with allusions to drug culture as in Cab Calloway's "Have You Seen That Funny Reefer Man?" "Plastered in Paris," or Fats Waller's "Viper's Drag" (a "viper" was slang for a marijuana smoker). A more recent example of a lyric with drug imagery is "Wacky Dust" as recorded by Manhattan Transfer.

*Rhyme*

Syncopation naturally has a lot to do with typical jazz rhyme and meter, and good jazz lyricists recognize the power of syncopation in both the music and the lyric of a song. Since typical jazz meter and rhythm are often sophisticated, jazz lyrics can sometimes be fairly wordy or esoteric. Here, the use of rhyme can help to tie the lyric together, as in the opening phrase of Cole Porter's jazzy "Anything Goes."

> *In olden days a glimpse of stocking,*
> *Was looked on as something shocking.*

Clever use of rhyming helps tie together the internal lyrics of the jazz-influenced song entitled "All for the Best" by Stephen Schwartz from the Broadway musical *Godspell*.

> *Some men are born to live at ease*
> *Doing what they please*
> *Richer than the bees are in honey.*

Rhyming is not essential in jazz songs that feature a strong, regular rhythm, like a bossa nova or a samba. The rhythm of the first lines of "Girl from Ipanema" is so consistent that the lyrics do not feature any rhyme.

> *Tall and tan and young and lovely,*
> *The girl from Ipanema goes walking.*

In a similar way, the jazz standard "Moonlight in Vermont" permits the absence of rhyme in its impressionistic portrait of a romantic woodland evening.

When coming up with rhymes for your own jazz lyrics, feel free to create internal rhymes where the rhythm of the music suggests them. Keep in mind that perfect rhymes and multiple rhyming, as in the work of Cole Porter and the Gershwins, evoke the air of sophistication that characterized the jazz-influenced music of the Broadway era, and the very polished big band music of the thirties and forties. By contrast, the use of imperfect rhymes will lend a freer, more earthy feeling to jazz lyrics, invoking the jazz music of the early days and the more recent Latin and modern jazz idioms.

## The Music of Jazz

The rhythmic, harmonic, and especially melodic particulars of the style have come from the outpourings of its more prominent practitioners. Although many jazz standards were borrowed (or, rather, forcibly adopted) from the realm of musical theater and other forms of popular music, this has always been a two-way street. The musical innovations of jazz have influenced every style of music being written today.

*The Jazz Melody*

While many jazz standards have very simple melodies, making them prime material for the improviser's embellishment, a jazz song written today should contain some characteristic idioms.

Jazz improvisers use a variety of scales and techniques to create uniquely jazz-sounding melodies, and so can the songwriter. One simple way to inject a jazz flavor into a melody is to base it on a *modal scale*. The *modes* are obtained by starting a major scale on a note other than its root. This rearranges the typical order of whole and half steps, creating a whole new flavor. If you take a C Major scale pattern and play it from D to D, you have played a D Dorian scale.

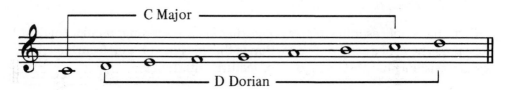

This type of modal melody was popularized by players like Miles Davis, Gerry Mulligan, and others during the fifties and sixties. Here are a few Dorian-mode riffs:

Other scales that can lend a particularly jazzy touch are the *diminished, whole-tone,* and *altered* scales. These are used to imply tensions in the harmony.

### Typical Jazz Progressions

The mainstay of the typical (and even of the not-so-typical) jazz chord progression is the II V I sequence. The numbers II V I refer to the chords built on the second, fifth, and first (or root) degrees of the scale. For example, in the key of C, II V I would indicate the chords D Minor, G, and C. Since jazz harmony makes extensive use of *higher number* chords—6s, 7s, 9s, 11s, and 13s—and *altered* chords—flat-5, sharp-5, flat-9, sharp-9, and sharp-11—this simple II V I progression might be voiced as follows:

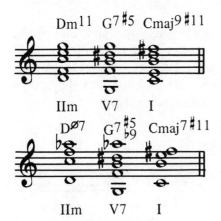

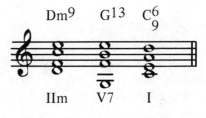

The II V I sequence provides a strong yet subtle way to establish a new key. Jazz songs frequently use the device of wandering through several keys (known as *transitory modulation*) to give them a characteristic harmonic interest and movement. This movement comes from the fact that the II chord in any key is the V of the V chord, and so provides the same strong pull toward the V that the V does toward the I. Using this reasoning, jazz writers often employ the V of the II chord in front of the sequence to turn it into a VI II V I. This example is based on the often-copied chord progression that Jerome Kern used in "All the Things You Are."

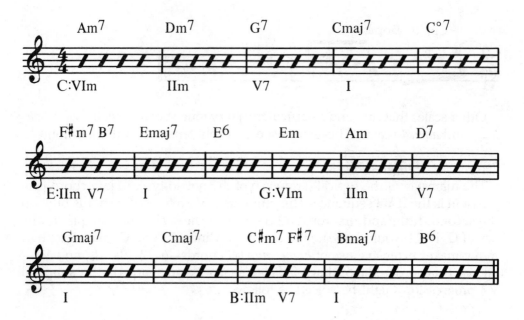

In the standard AABA form, a II V I sequence is often used to establish the bridge section in a new key. Sometimes the new key is a *related* key, one built from a scale degree of the original key (usually the IV, V, or VI). In Hoagy Carmichael's "Two Sleepy People," the A sections are in E-flat and the bridge modulates (changes key) to A-flat (the key of the IV chord).

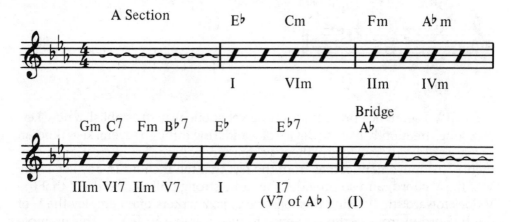

The power of the II V sequence comes in handy when the bridge is moving to an *unrelated* key. This is often the case in jazz songs because the farther away from the key of the A sections you take the bridge, the more interesting the progression must be to get back to the original key. Consider this bridge similar to "Body and Soul" and how it manages to return to the original key of C from the unrelated key of D-flat.

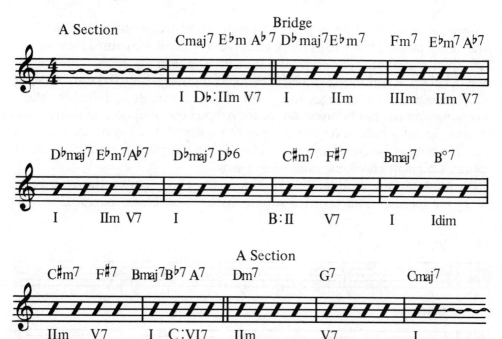

## Rhythm and Tempo

As far as rhythm is concerned, jazz is about syncopation and swing but, as with melody, the rhythm of a jazz song should also feature straight rhythms for the sake of contrast. Often the syncopation occurs in a question or answer phrase paired with a straighter phrase. Consider the rhythm of the opening bars of Louis Armstrong's theme song "When It's Sleepy-Time Down South."

Another good example would be the old chestnut "Pennies from Heaven."

Taken as a whole, jazz is predominantly an instrumental music, and instrumental jazz typically uses more elaborate rhythmic structures than songs. This rhythmic complexity reached a frenetic height in the 1940s with the advent of bebop. A common practice of bebop composers was to take an old song with interesting chord changes and give it a hip new melody and rhythm. Many jazz songs are written in imitation, or from direct transcription, of instrumental jazz. To get a handle on these types of rhythms, it is a good idea to do a lot of listening to the great jazz players like Dizzy Gillespie, Charlie Parker, Lester Young, Coleman Hawkins, and Miles Davis.

The most important underlying rhythm in most jazz songs is the *swing* beat. Swing is a specific variation on the shuffle rhythm (see "Blues," pages 115 to 125).

In a band situation, this beat is generally laid down by the drummer on the high hat or cymbal, but even if it is not obvious, it is usually felt in the music. The swing beat forces a song's rhythm into a triplet feel.

Note that you will seldom see jazz rhythms notated as accurately as they are here. They are usually simplified to make them easier to read, with the assumption that the performer will provide the swing.

The intricacy of jazz music itself can make it tough to get lyrics that work well. Since jazz is primarily an instrumental music, it is usually up to the lyricist to make the compromises and adjustments when it comes to putting it all together. Sometimes to frame and support a particularly wild jazz song, the lyric must be quite imagistic and even erratic. But when you've made a good match, both melody and lyric should seem to emerge together, as if they are both coming out of the same saxophone.

# 11

# The Black Sound—
# From Rhythm and Blues to Rap

*A big hit would get right into the jukebox in the ice cream store, you know? And the elite suburban parents didn't want the kids to even hear it. They'd call the radio stations and say, "Don't play that record! We've got the kids dancing to it!"*

—Chuck Berry

*In my days of flaming youth I was extremely suspect of any rock music played by white people. The sincerity and emotional intensity of their performances, when they sang, about boyfriends and girl friends and breaking up etc., was nowhere when I compared it to my high school Negro R&B heroes like Johnny Otis, Howlin' Wolf, and Willie Mae Thornton.*

—Frank Zappa

## The Black American Musical Tradition

The course of American popular music has been directed by the work of black artists and songwriters from its early beginnings. In the nineteenth century, black work songs and the dance music of southern plantations gave birth to the blues. The early blues and the ragtime music of black vaudeville and minstrel shows laid the foundations for modern jazz, and black spirituals paved the way for modern gospel music. Euro-American musical traditions were integral to the growth of popular American music as well, but the black American influence was the prime mover of these musical styles, particularly at their inception.

Through the decades, the music of black artists and songwriters has been referred to collectively by many terms. In the early days, these recordings were called "race records." Then the term "rhythm and blues" was used to describe the non-jazz blues band sound that remained popular into the seventies. A wide variety of black musical styles today don't fall naturally into the categories of the pop charts. These include songs that are pure renditions of rap, funk, disco, and soul. So *Billboard* now has a chart for "Black Hits," to include the material in these special styles. When you think about it, the music of black artists has always been characterized by diverse musical styles—even before the recording industry was born.

## The Birth of Rhythm and Blues

Rhythm and blues grew out of the various kinds of urban blues popular in the early part of this century, particularly the dance hall blues and boogie-woogie styles. The first blues recordings were made in the twenties, and songs like Mamie Smith's 1920 version of "Crazy Blues" and the recordings of artists like Robert Johnson and Mississippi John Hurt were regarded by the early recording industry as ethnic or novelty songs. By the 1920s, a few independent record companies (and specialty-label divisions of the majors) were formed that specialized in the work of black artists; these recordings were aimed primarily at the black listener. At that time, these recordings were not categorized according to a particular musical style, such as jazz or blues. During the thirties, some of this blues-based music developed a distinctive dance rhythm and a driving band instrumentation, and rhythm and blues was born. The typical R&B ensemble featured saxophone, harmonica, piano, guitar, and drums in bold, hard-edged arrangements. The advent of the microphone and the electric guitar helped to strengthen the already powerful vocals and instrumentals characteristic of the style.

## Jazz and Rhythm and Blues

During the forties, black big bands performed both the jazz/swing and the dance blues sound. In the later part of the decade, these bands began to specialize. So the two main commercial venues for the black performer were jazz and the much newer style, rhythm and blues. At the time, many black artists felt that the tastes of the white listening audience had brought a kind of polish to jazz that took the life or maybe just the fun out of the more rhythmic, improvisational jazz of the previous decades. Artists like Duke Ellington who featured the orchestral jazz sound were more marketable to both the black and the white listener. The music of bandleaders like Tiny Bradshaw and Buddy Johnson, which featured the driving R&B sound, were enjoyed mainly by black audiences. By the time R&B artists like Fats Domino and Lloyd Price came along, the white listener was ready for the exciting new sound, and by the early fifties the white audience had increased considerably. Rhythm and blues developed as a distinctive musical style and became the new thrust of black popular music. The acceptance of this tough, rhythmic sound also laid the groundwork for the birth of rock and roll—the child of R&B and country music.

## The Black Sound Today

Beginning in the seventies, innovators like Sly Stone brought rhythm and blues into the pop charts. Although rhythm and blues is still a distinctive type of music, it no longer has its own chart of hit songs, but shares the black hit chart with the disco, rap, soul, and pop tunes of black artists. These other musical styles are, to different extents, actually offshoots of rhythm and blues. In fact, popular music in general, especially rock and pop, may be said to have developed under the direct influence of R&B music. Soul, Motown, and funk are part of the R&B family, and even disco is a cousin of the style.

### Soul

In the early seventies, the term *rhythm and blues* began to seem old-fashioned. In the slick world of the record industry, the designation sounded decidedly down-home and not a little incongruous to be applied to performers who had come a long way from the blues. In keeping with the black power and black pride movements of the day, the new term "soul music" was chosen as the official title (although this name had been used for some time previously). The new name also seemed more apt for performers like Al Green and Aretha Franklin who were bringing the emotionally charged performance techniques of black gospel to the ears of the listening public.

Throughout the seventies and eighties, soul has continued to evolve, building on its R&B roots and incorporating thematic and musical elements of jazz, rock, pop, and Latin music. In turn, many songs by black performers (including Stevie Wonder, Tina Turner, and Michael Jackson) now routinely cross over to the pop and rock charts.

### Gospel

Religious music has been an important part of black American life since the early part of the nineteenth century. When the blues became a rhythmic dance form around the turn of the century, the spiritual also blossomed into a more rhythmic form and gospel was born. Artists like Mahalia Jackson and James Cleveland, and gospel groups like the Dixie Hummingbirds, Mitchell's Christian Singers, and the Five Blind Boys of Mississippi made the first modern gospel recordings. At times, gospel was referred to as soul music, but this term gradually came to refer to rhythm and blues, and to black music in general.

Today white and black gospel music is still very much alive in the work of artists like Amy Grant and André Crouch. Although these strains of gospel-rock and gospel-influenced pop music are part of today's scene, many gospel purists and old-timers have always been quite proud of the distinctive character of this musical style. Legendary gospel artist Mahalia Jackson put it this way: "I like nothing better than to defend my personal belief that gospel songs in my repertory are not blues, not jazz, and in fact not spirituals."

## Funk

Funk is a direct outgrowth of the driving R&B dance tradition of the fifties and sixties. The advent of sophisticated synthesizers and drum machines brought the already-strong groove and rhythm of the style to a fevered pitch. George Clinton's groups Parliament and Funkadelic were frontrunners of funk in the seventies and Clinton is still turning out dance hits like "Atomic Dog." Rick James also created some important funk hits in the seventies and eighties like "Give It to Me Baby" and "Super Freak." Funk lyrics often are quite abstract, for, as George Clinton said, "You cannot make sense and be funky. We take the heaviness out of being profound."

Today, funk is alive and well in the work of such artists as Jimmy Jam, Terry Lewis, and Prince. The rapid improvement of synthesizers and the computerized recording studio help songwriters get that funky sound. If you are interested in writing funk music and aren't at home in the recording studio, it's a good idea to team up with someone knowledgeable about synthesizers and rhythm machines or get familiar with them yourself. Funk is one style of music where production values and technical know-how are truly essential to successful songwriting.

## Disco

Disco emerged in the early seventies as a powerful dance music. Although conceived primarily by black artists, white artists and writers shared in its early growth. Hits like Hues Corporation's "Rock the Boat" and KC and the Sunshine Band's "Blow Your Whistle" and "Get Down Tonight" made it on the pop charts in the mid-seventies. Van McCoy's "The Hustle" really started the disco dance rage that continued full force into the eighties. The Bee Gees scored a disco smash with their double album soundtrack to the movie *Saturday Night Fever* with the number one hits "Stayin' Alive" and "Night Fever." In 1977, the group A Taste of Honey received a Grammy as "Best New Artist" for their number one disco hit "Boogie Oogie Oogie." By the late seventies, disco as a phenomenon had faded, but the actual style had not. The elements of disco had simply been incorporated into pop and rock. Many current albums rely heavily on the fundamentals of disco.

### Reggae

Reggae developed in Jamaica as an outgrowth of soul and funk filtered through calypso and other West Indian traditions. The purest form of reggae draws its inspiration from the mystic Jah religion, centered on Haile Selassie and other cult figures. While the recordings of artists such as U Roy, Burning Spear, and Bob Marley continue to enjoy great popularity, reggae's lasting impact is probably the rhythmic influence it has had on all forms of popular music since the early seventies.

### Rap

It was the black disk jockeys and reggae "dub artists" of the late seventies who really started rap by adding witty comments and rhyming phrases as they spun the funk hits. This led to the remixing of current hits to feature the DJ throughout. Record jockeys like DJ Hollywood, and reggae dub artists like Cool Herc, began to feature fully fledged rap songs in live performance. James Brown's "Get Up, Get Into It, Get Involved" was a rap-oriented cut that also helped to start things off. Soon original music was substituted for remixed funk tunes, and rap became a form of its own.

Today Run DMC, Whodini, and a host of other rappers enjoy popular success. Their themes range from traditional teen rebellion to rather high-minded raps of advice and admonition. Although rap artists use musical intonations and melodic phrasing, rap is not actually a song form because there is no real melody. The "lyrics" are spoken, not sung.

### Rhythm and Blues and Soul Themes

Rhythm and blues and soul songs traditionally deal with themes of an adult nature. Love and desire have always been favorites, with an emphasis on sexuality and deep emotional attachments. Since R&B arose from early blues dance music, many songs deal with dancing and the nature of rhythm itself. Another theme inherited from the blues is that of human dissolution: having the blues. As R&B started to cross over to the pop charts in the 1950s, and white teenagers started listening, the songs eased up on adult themes. The more mature expressions of love or anguish gave way to themes of romance and the difficulties and joys faced by the younger listener. Today's R&B and soul lyrics often focus on rhythm and dancing, often in view of their power to reveal the joy of living and loving through movement.

### Gospel Themes

Technically, every gospel song must center on one theme: the redeeming power of Jesus Christ. Early black spirituals sometimes dealt with the power of Christ, but more often with the wonders of the Old Testament and the Almighty. Pure gospel songs often name the Savior and celebrate the mutual love of God and man. Rock-gospel themes are a bit more far-reaching, with an emphasis on spiritual uplift and religious feelings in a more general sense.

### Funk and Disco Themes

Being primarily music for dancing, both the disco song of the seventies and that of the resurgence of the eighties naturally employs themes that revolve around rhythm and the dance itself, the disco scene, and dancing. Funk music often deals with these same themes, with perhaps more emphasis on love and lovemaking.

### Rhythm and Blues and Soul Titles

Such early soul and R&B titles as "Chains of Love," "Lovin' Machine," and "I Want a Bow-Legged Woman" were typical of the highly charged and explicit treatment of romance. More innocent romantic themes are expressed in "Lipstick, Powder and Paint" and "Sweet Sixteen." Though R&B cooled a bit on sexual themes in the fifties and sixties, the pains of lost love were still strongly stated in songs like "Teardrops from My Eyes" and "Love Don't Love Nobody." Traditional blues themes about hard luck and the downside of life are still mainstays of the genre. Classic titles of this kind include "Hard Luck Blues" and "Drifting from Town to Town."

### Gospel Titles

The gospel title inevitably refers to its sole theme—salvation—as attained directly through the figure of Jesus Christ. Some recent "pure" gospel titles include André Crouch's "I Have Got a Savior" and Rev. F. C. Barnes and Rev. Janice Brown's "I Hear Jesus Calling." Some of the freer or "less-sacred" gospel titles have enjoyed more commercial success, as with James Brown's "Please, Please, Please" and Marvin Gaye's "Can I Get a Witness." Choosing a gospel title can be tricky because if you go for the conservative, "sacred" title, you please the churchiest of the gospel listeners, but you lose many of the more liberal gospel and R&B fans. On the other hand, if you go with the more secular gospel title, you're more apt to please the commercial crowd and lose the gospel purists. The best gospel titles reach both of these groups by finding a way to include the Savior and his powers in the title without sounding too old-fashioned.

### Funk and Disco Titles

Rhythm and Blues has always focused on dance and rhythm, with titles like "Good Rockin' Tonight" and "Boogie at Midnight." Rhythm is also a favorite theme of funk titles as well, like "One Nation Under a Groove," "Walking in Rhythm," and "Hit Me with Your Rhythm Stick." The groove and the driving beat of this brand of music is embodied in the meaning of the word funk itself—"Funkytown," "Play That Funky Music," and "Funky Stuff." If you choose a title that suggests that your tune is funky, be sure that the musical elements of the song live up to that claim, especially the rhythm.

The disco of the seventies had titles that pointed up its distinctive new rhythm and danceability. "You Should Be Dancing" and "Boogie Child" by the Bee Gees and Chic's "Dance, Dance, Dance (Yowsah, Yowsah, Yowsah)" are just a few of the many disco titles that stress this theme. Some titles, like Johnnie Taylor's "Disco Lady" and the Trammps' "Disco Inferno" mention the style itself. Since dance and romance often go together, love (especially its physical expressions) is also a common theme for the disco title. Artists like Donna Summer went a long way with sexy disco titles like "Love to Love You Baby" and many imitators followed with titles about lovemaking, such as Andrea Love Connection's "More, More, More." There were some successful novelty titles too, like Carl Douglas's "Kung Fu Fighting," designed to inspire dancers to mimic the martial arts while disco dancing.

Rhythm, dance, and love are themes featured in all styles of black dance music, from rhythm and blues to disco. But if you're planning to write about more down-to-earth human emotions and situations, it's a good idea to stick with soul and rhythm and blues, where this kind of title is more commonplace. Disco and funk rarely have the time to go into detail about human relationships, so, these titles should be exciting and simple.

## The Lyric of the Black Sound

Rhythm and blues and soul lyrics have always focused on powerful human emotions, usually as expressed from one person's point of view. Lyrics typically feature strong metrical phrasing. The very regular beat of the lyric is complemented by free-flowing language and the speaker's conversational tone. Since love is so often the theme, complex rhyming seems appropriate and also serves to point up the regularity of the beat. As the R&B song's melody and harmony are usually regular, it's important that the lyric be exciting and catchy, and that they work well with the song's rhythmic elements to create an inviting groove. Usually the chorus is quite simple and features the hook in repetition, while the lyric of the verse provides details and imagery that set the stage for the main theme. The Temptations' recent success "Lady Soul," by Mark Holden, typifies the theme of love in today's soul lyric. The verse section sets up the two characters in an openly romantic setting.

> *Lying here beside you*
> *Close as we can be*
> *I know what this leads to*
> *I know what you need.*
>
> *I'm ready to surrender my love*
> *Lay it all in your hands*
> *Give you my forever*
> *Everything I am.*

Although "what this leads to" and "what you need" suggest the act of lovemaking itself, here physical love and spiritual love are practically inseparable. Through the act of love, the speaker feels he will be able to express the enduring and complete qualities of his feelings. Soul and R&B songs more often portray love and loving from an adult perspective than do the more youth-oriented black pop and funk.

Notice that the individual lines of the lyric are short and to the point. There are no distracting details. It is enough to know that two characters are lying close to each other, love each other, and are about to consummate that fact. Although the song is really about lovemaking, the subject is handled with warmth and a certain delicacy. Here euphemisms like "surrender my love" and "give you my forever" help to get the message across with sincerity and taste. The chorus reflects on the lady's importance in the singer's life and her love's positive effects.

> *'Cause you are my, my, my, my lady soul*
> *You warm my heart*
> *When I grow cold*
> *Oh you are my, my, my, my lady soul*
> *You are my life*
> *You make me whole*
> *O-o-o-o*
> *O-o-o-o*
> *My lady soul.*

The hook is repeated three times in the chorus and the repetition of the word "my" or "o" before the hook serves to emphasize its importance. The intimate bedroom setting of the verse is contrasted here with a more philosophical view of love and its spiritual benefits, a theme which is well-captured in the hook phrase, "Lady Soul."

As you are developing your own lyrics, keep a strong and regular rhythmic pattern in mind. Don't hesitate to let a single line of lyric express one complete idea; this is a trademark of today's soul and R&B lyrics. The language you use should be natural and straightforward, and delivered by a motivated speaker in conversational tones.

While R&B and soul are directed toward the adult listener, funk and disco lyrics are generally intended for a younger audience. Colloquialisms and nonsense-syllables are often featured in the typical funk lyrics. The repetition of humorous and suggestive ideas help to make the lyric sound hip. Janet Jackson's "Nasty" by James Harris II and Terry Lewis is characteristic of funk's deceptive simplicity and sassy sense of fun.

> *I don't like no nasty girl*
> *I don't like no nasty food*
> *The only nasty thing I like is the nasty groove.*

The paradoxical meaning of the word "nasty," surely a descendant of "bad," is clear. Nasty girls and food are one thing, but the groove of Janet's song is so "nasty," it's terrific.

When writing your own funk lyric, it pays to take one catch phrase or mood and carry it through to the end. R&B and soul are much better vehicles for lyrics that feature dimensional themes, imagery, and detail.

### The Black American Vocabulary

Just as black music has been a guiding force in the development of popular music, so black American speech and the lyrics of black writers have done much to shape the overall character of popular song lyrics.

Rhythm and Blues and soul lyrics often contain informal spellings and Southernisms: "burnin' " for "burning," "wanna" for "want to," "c'mon," " 'cause," and "I got." These contractions are now mainstays of rock and pop music. You'll probably find that a judicious use of informal pronunciation and phrasing can make lyrics sound hip. Popular black slang is evolving all the time. Yesterday's "get down" may be today's "chill." There are subtle differences between "groovin'," "freakin'," and "jammin'," and what was once "bad" is now "nasty." Talk to people that are up on the slang in vogue, and choose your words carefully. Don't overdo it: most songs only use one or two jive words each, and these are usually repeated.

### Imagery

The black sound takes much of its imagery from life. As in pop and rock, the song is often set on the dance floor, in the street, or in the privacy of home. Since love is so often the theme, visions of a loved one or a potential loved one are almost always the focus. There's the Controllers' "Distant Lover," Chico DeBarge's "The Girl Next Door," and Rick James's "Sweet and Sexy Thing." Often the imagery centers on a metaphor for love, as in Klymaxx's "Man Size Love" or Billy Ocean's "Love Zone."

Elevated states of mind and social and spiritual identity are often expressed through imagery. "Mountains" by Prince and the Revolution uses natural images to express love's durability. Chaka Khan's "Earth to Micki" uses a spaceship to illustrate the main character's high energy and unattainability. When writing your own R&B-influenced lyrics, you may use fairly creative imagery, but be sure the images you choose are powerful and clear in relation to the song's main theme.

### Rhyme

Rhyme and rhyming sounds are very important in R&B and its related styles, for they reinforce the song's inherent rhythm and movement and lend a polished and even prophetic quality to the song's message.

It's almost impossible to use too much rhyme in funk lyrics; in fact, sometimes elegant rhyming seems more important than meaning. Rhythm and blues and soul also feature frequent rhymes and rhymelike sounds to emphasize the song's form and rhythm, and to clarify its message.

## The Music of the Black Sound

Although the terms "R&B" and "soul" were used during the fifties, sixties, and early seventies to designate any music by black artists or for black audiences, there are nonetheless musical factors that make these identifiable song genres. The ballad forms of R&B and soul take many of their rhythmic ideas from the blues; making ample use of the $\frac{6}{4}$ meter with a backbeat (listen to Sam Cooke's "You Send Me" or "When a Man Loves a Woman" by Percy Sledge). It is in the uptunes that the "rhythm" of rhythm and blues comes into play. Songs like Wilson Pickett's "Midnight Hour" make use of straight $\frac{4}{4}$ meter (as opposed to the $\frac{12}{8}$ shuffle of the blues) but with recurring, syncopated patterns that create an urgent yet controlled movement. One of the basic rhythmic patterns that appears in "Midnight Hour" also turns up, with slight variations, in countless R&B and soul hits, including Eddie Floyd's "Knock on Wood," Smokey Robinson's "Get Ready," and Martha Reeves and the Vandellas' "Dancing in the Street."

In early R&B songs, the melodic ideas came directly from the blues. Today, the actual melody of the song often bears more resemblance to a pop-rock melody, with most of the blues and gospel influences originating in the performer's interpretation. Many soul melodies are made up entirely of notes within the major scale, such as Otis Redding's "(Sittin' on the) Dock of the Bay," the Temptations' "Ain't' Too Proud to Beg," or of notes from the minor scale, such as Bill Withers's "Ain't No Sunshine" and the Four Tops' "Standing in the Shadows of Love."

In many cases, the scales used in constructing the melodies are influenced by complex chord changes incorporating sophisticated harmonic devices such as modulations to related and unrelated keys, altered chords, and chord substitutions. Starting with the highly arranged Motown Sound of the sixties, the chord progressions of many soul tunes began to demonstrate an intricacy that approached that of jazz. However, the recent revival of such songs as Bill Withers's 1972 hit "Lean on Me" and Marvin Gaye's 1968 "I Heard It Through the Grapevine" demonstrates the power of the unadorned, blues/gospel-influenced chord progression and melody. Notice the unaffected I IV V simplicity of "Lean on Me:"

The disco of the seventies relied for the most part on the simple rhythmic device of eight eighth notes or sixteen sixteenth notes per measure, making it adaptable to almost any type of fast dancing.

The melodies were most often derived from the minor and blues scales. Disco melody, harmony, and rhythm create an overall sense of perpetual motion through the use of marked repetitions. The groove never seems to stop.

Disco today has largely been absorbed by pop and rock music, but has enjoyed a recent resurgence as a distinctive musical style, particularly in the Latin market, where it is still popular as a pure dance form.

Similarly, what goes by the name of funk must be danceable, but it is distinguished by decidedly more complex rhythms. But, even though the rhythms are complex, their complexity comes from the subdivision of the basic $\frac{4}{4}$ meter. Here is how you might subdivide the beat in a typical funk song.

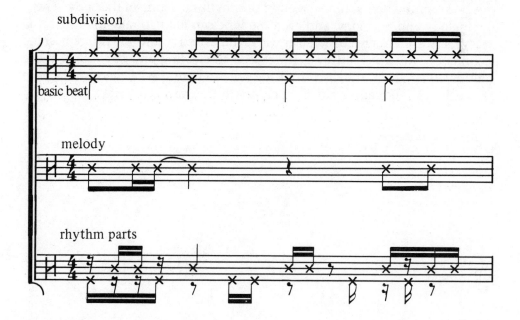

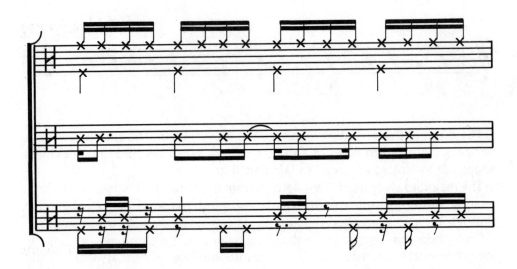

Whether you are writing funk, disco, or up-tempo rhythm and blues, keep in mind that danceability is a deciding factor of a song's success in these genres. Even in slower ballads, the underlying rhythm is of paramount importance. You might find it easiest to design the musical elements of your song around a particularly interesting or exciting groove or feel. A drum machine or sequencer can be helpful when you are creating the rhythmic fabric of the song. Then, the melody and harmony, and even the lyric can fall naturally into the same groove. If you aren't already familiar with synthesized sound and drum machine techniques, you'll benefit by getting used to creating and controlling these sounds. Again, funk and disco-funk are styles where special effects and studio pyrotechnics can really make a difference in the way you write a song.

# 12

# Country and Western

*You ask me what makes our kind of music successful. I'll tell you. It can be explained in just one word: sincerity.*

—Hank Williams

*I have no desire to write pop songs. I love country music. If one of my songs goes pop, I'm tickled to death. It's a bonus.*

—Harlan Howard

## The American Folk Tradition

Early colonists brought the musical styles of their homelands to America. The popular ballad song form and the rich fiddling traditions of Europe, particularly of Britain, laid the groundwork for American folk music. The southern Appalachian region was especially fertile ground for America's earliest music. Rural dance and song traditions became an integral part of the lives of the people of the American South and West. As the population of the new country grew, its music took on a distinct American flavor, as it was enriched by the contributions of many cultures. Perhaps the most important of these contributions was the influence of the rich Afro-American musical tradition, which was also developing simultaneously. By 1900, the raucous sound of the square dance stringband, the joyous strains of the white gospel songs and hymns (largely an adaptation of the black spiritual), and the high, lonesome sound of the solo ballad singer accompanying himself on the five-string banjo were heard throughout the South. With the help of improved mass communication offered by radio and the phonograph, the music of the South began to emerge as a popular genre.

### The Nation Discovers Hillbilly Music

Many historians trace the beginning of popular country music to 1902 when Len Spenser recorded the fiddle song "Arkansas Traveler" for Thomas Edison. During the early years of the twentieth century, Tin Pan Alley songwriters recognized the commercial value of what came to be known as "hillbilly" and "cowboy" songs, which they considered novelty or "eccentric" numbers. Honky-tonk songs began appearing on Tin Pan Alley, and in the twenties such tunes as "Sister Honky-Tonk" and "Honky-Tonk Train Blues" were popular. Although these do not qualify as country songs, early honky-tonk and boogie-woogie influenced the country music of the later thirties and forties, when country musicians developed their own brand of honky-tonk music typified by the songs of Ernest Tubb and Hank Williams.

By the twenties, this novelty music came to be recognized as a true style, and the first stars of country music emerged. Artists like Uncle Dave Macon, the Carter Family, and, most notably, Jimmie Rodgers commanded national attention. In 1925, radio station WSM began broadcasting a hillbilly music show called the WSM Barn Dance, the title of which was soon changed to the Grand Ole Opry. Nashville, Tennessee, was on its way to becoming the commercial center of country and western music.

### Country and Western Comes into Its Own

Throughout the Swing Era, country and western music continued to grow and develop. It became a chiefly vocal music, with an emphasis on the solo singer in a small band setting. The instrumentation still featured the traditional fiddles and guitars, but with the addition of piano, bass, drums, and a new instrument, the electric steel guitar. In Oklahoma and Texas, country and western performers started to incorporate elements of jazz into their playing and arrangements, and western swing was born. Western swing bands such as Bob Wills and His Texas Playboys went so far as to employ a full swing big band instrumentation with brass and reed sections, not unlike those of the Benny Goodman or Artie Shaw orchestras.

The Southwest at this time also saw the rise of the small-band type of music called honky-tonk. Honky-tonk gave country music its pervasive themes of barrooms and drinking, cheating (and sex), and high times in general. In the Southeast, another offshoot developed that looked backward to more traditional forms for its roots: bluegrass. Bluegrass was and is more instrumentally oriented than most country music, and while honky-tonk, western swing, and mainstream country music were making extensive use of the newly developed electric guitar, bluegrass remained staunchly acoustic, featuring a new style of five-string banjo picking developed by Earl Scruggs with Bill Monroe and the Blue Grass Boys, along with Monroe's distinctive high tenor vocals and rhythmic mandolin style.

### Country Music Today: The Nashville Sound

Since the mid-sixties there has existed a phenomenon known as the "Nashville Sound." While it has always been met with much critical derision, it has nevertheless always been commercially successful. What producers like Owen Bradley, Billy Sherrill, and Jerry Kennedy did was to apply pop techniques—string sections, "ooh-ah" backup vocals, prominent drum tracks, and plenty of reverb—to material that still resonated with traditional country music themes.

Any such radical innovation within a music community either is a flash in the pan or, as happened with the Nashville Sound, is more or less gradually accepted and establishes a tradition of its own. By the mid-seventies, it seemed as if this "countrypolitan" sound would eclipse all other forms of country music. Within recent years, artists like Ricky Scaggs, Emmylou Harris, George Strait, Dwight Yokum, and Vince Gill have proved that a wide market still exists for the traditional honky-tonk, western swing, and rockabilly styles.

## The Many Faces of Country and Western

These different styles continue to exist side by side under the collective heading of country music mainly because of the nature of the audience. Country fans tend to be extremely loyal, enabling country artists to enjoy careers that span decades. (Roy Acuff, for example, joined the Grand Ole Opry in 1938 and is still one of its mainstays.) Also, the themes of nostalgia and the simple life are naturally expressed in the musical styles as well as the lyrics of the songs.

This is not to say that the field is stagnant or backward. From the beginning, country has embraced (somewhat grudgingly at times) innovations from blues, rock, swing, pop, and even soul and disco. Many country hits today achieve such crossover success that rock and pop listeners are unaware that they are hearing a song by a "country" artist. For the songwriter, this leaves the field wide open: the established genres are there, but a little (or a lot) of blurring at the edges is acceptable.

## Country and Western Themes

Country and western music takes its name from the southern and western regions of the United States where it emerged. Thus, the bulk of country music deals with themes relevant to rural and city life in these regions. Like all other popular music styles today, the joys and difficulties of love is a favorite theme of country music. Often there is a story or explanation of why the lovers are parted and many times it's due to infidelity, separation, or self-destructive behavior. Thus drinking, gambling, cheating, hell-raising, and breaking the law are often central themes of the story.

Paradoxically, the upstanding themes of patriotism, happy home life and children, and devotion to God are nearly as popular as those dealing with the downside of life. While not nearly as prevalent as other types of country songs on the charts, true gospel songs do turn up now and then, and country artists often include both cheating songs and gospel songs on the same album.

## The Country Title

The country title does not hesitate to be lengthy if the theme requires it. Titles like "Don't Leave Without Taking Your Silver" and "My Old Flame Is Burnin' Another Honky-Tonk Down" are examples of the full phrasing that characterizes quite a few country tunes. Short descriptive titles are effective too—as in "Faded Love" and "Big City." Be sure that your country titles are relatively simple and straightforward, but don't worry if it takes a few words to illustrate the theme.

Some country titles center on an aspect of the music itself, as in "Play Me Some Mountain Music," "Rhythm of the Road," "If You Want to Play in Texas, You've Got to Have a Fiddle in the Band." Many country and western titles commemorate the name of a particular southern state or region, like "Texas When I Die," and "Louisiana Woman, Mississippi Man." Other titles deal with some aspect of the rural landscape, like "That Georgia Sun Was Blood Red and Going Down." The industrial South and West provide titles for songs like "Coal Tattoo" and "One Piece at a Time," Johnny Cash's story of a factory worker who steals a car from the assembly line "one piece at a time." Employment problems and hard luck also appear in many country titles—"Take This Job and Shove It," "A Working Man Can't Get Nowhere Today," and "Are the Good Times Really Over for Good?" Sometimes the confrontation of city and country life is expressed in a song title—as in Glen Campbell's "Country Boy (You Got Your Feet in L.A.)" and Hank Williams, Jr.'s "A Country Boy Can Survive."

Naturally love and romance often appear in titles, like "You're My Best Friend," "I Love," and "It Must Be Love." Loneliness and love's disappointments may even be more common, as in "Sea of Heartbreak," "Ashes of Love," or "You Never Looked That Good When You Were Mine." Family life and broken families are also common title themes for country tunes like "I've Got a Darling for a Wife," "I'm the Only Hell (Mama Ever Raised)," "Mama Tried," and "D-I-V-O-R-C-E."

The pleasures and pains of alcohol, gambling, and sleeping around are expressed in titles such as "Honky-Tonk Crazy," "Swinging Doors," "That Girl Who Waits on Tables Used to Wait for Me at Home," "Don't Cheat in Our Hometown," "Your Cheating Heart," "Kentucky Gambler," and "Gambling Polka-Dot Blues." Many country songs are portraits of a single character—"Delta Dawn," "The Queen of the Silver Dollar," and "Daddy Was a Hardworking, Honest Man."

Other, more upbeat titles stress the themes of patriotism—"Red Necks, White Socks, and Blue Ribbon Beer," "God Bless the USA;" general good feeling and exuberation—"I'm the Happiest Girl in the Whole USA," "Born to Boogie;" or religion—"You Can't Be a Beacon if Your Light Don't Shine," "The Baptism of Jesse Taylor." Wordplay is often used to make a country title interesting and catchy. "Need a Little Time Off for Bad Behavior," "The Right Left Hand," and "You Can't Get the Hell Out of Texas" use clever turns of phrase to drive their message home. Metaphor and simile can be effective, too—as in "Tonight We're Going to Tear Down the Walls" or "Life's Like Poetry."

When choosing your own country and western titles, be sure that they express themes that would be appreciated by the average adult middle American. Although clever turns of phrase can make an image or a situation quite vivid, don't overcomplicate your title. If it's not straightforward and earthy, it won't reach the average country and western listener.

## The Country and Western Lyric

The simplicity of the typical country melody and harmony brings the lyric into sharp focus. Many times it is the lyric, rather than the music, that provides the song with different tones and colors. Although lyrics, too, should be relatively simple and straightforward, they often explore difficult emotional situations and touchingly realistic environments and moods. Country lyrics are often charged with sentiment and freely feature melodramatic events—particularly where love is concerned. The chorus of the George Jones hit, "He Stopped Loving Her Today," is a classic example of country sentimentality.

> *He stopped loving her today,*
> *They placed a wreath upon his door,*
> *And soon they'll carry him away.*
> *He stopped loving her today.*

This kind of raw sentiment would never wash in pop or rock lyrics, but in the country setting it is somehow sincere and touching. Randy Travis's "Forever and Ever, Amen" uses hyperbole to express the eternal quality of the speaker's love for his mate. In the chorus, the speaker insists that his love will last "as long as old men sit and talk about the weather" and "as long as old women sit and talk about old men." When writing your own lyrics about love themes, there's really no limit to how much you can romanticize the subject, as long as the expressions are sincere.

### The Story Song

Many country lyrics tell a story. It may be love story, a tale of adventure and fun, or a serious drama of injustice or retribution. Ricky Van Shelton's hit song "Crime of Passion" by Walt Aldridge and Mac McAnally is a good example of the dramatic country tale. Although in songs like these the speaker is often simply a narrator, here the speaker interacts in the plot. The first verse sets up the story's characters and events in vivid detail.

> She had a ragtop El Dorado
> Tuck and roll pleat
> She picked me up in Colorado
> And put me right in the driver's seat
> I said I got no money, I got no job
> She said I tell you what honey
> Let's find a place to rob.
> Now the man at the station's name was Jim
> I saw it sewed on his shirt
> I told him to do what I say
> You'll live another day
> Nobody's gotta get hurt.

In just twelve lines we learn how these partners in crime met, agreed to, and committed a robbery. Yet there's still time for realistic detail like the specific make and style of the woman's car, who drove, and the name embroidered on the gas station attendant's shirt. Dialogue between the characters also helps add to the drama. The chorus then gives us the hook and seems to sum up the characters' relationship and deeper motives in a nutshell.

> Crime of passion
> She took me by the heart
> When she took me by the hand
> Crime of passion
> A beautiful woman
> And a desperate man.

The second verse reveals the startling truth of the frame-up, and the true motive of his traitorous partner. As the chorus returns, the hook has a deeper meaning as the female character is now paired with her real partner in love and crime. Here the word "him" instead of "me" drives home the new meaning.

> *Well I thought the thing was over*
> *She was counting the cash*
> *When an unmarked Chevy Nova*
> *Made the blue lights flash*
> *She said officer won't you please help me*
>
> *I looked at her and she was pointing at me.*
> *You see Jim at the station played the part*
> *And I talked a little perjury*
> *He went to great pains*
> *To leave out her name*
> *He was her future ex-husband*
> *Can't you see.*
>
> *Crime of passion*
> *She took him by the heart*
> *When she took him by the hand*
> *Crime of passion*
> *A beautiful woman*
> *And a desperate man.*

Notice how the image of her counting the stolen cash and the specifics about the police car help bring the picture into focus. Again, dialogue highlights the dramatic quality of the event:

> *Now the man at the station's name was Joe*
> *I saw it on the badge on his shirt*
> *He said you'll never get away*
> *But do what we say*
> *And nobody has to get hurt.*

This last partial verse is a clever play on the events of the robbery. Instead of a gas station, it is a police station. The authoritative voice is no longer the speaker but the policeman, who ironically echoes the words spoken at the holdup. Again, the speaker is able to identify a character by name by reading it off his shirt. The second version of the chorus then repeats again to drive home the theme of treachery and violence, born of passion. This clear metaphorical comparison of the speaker's paradoxical relationship to the victim/victimizer, "Jim," the deceptive yet "beautiful woman," and the strong arm of the law, "Joe," give the story a compelling layer of double meanings. We are left with the feeling that the events of the story have a larger message regarding the changing face of love and justice, and the cyclic and retributive nature of human fate. That's a lot to get from a song that lasts just a few short minutes.

When writing songs of this type, be sure to give each character a good reason for appearing in the story. Pick a few details that help the listener visualize the events as they occur. In general, have each verse provide a new chapter in the story. This will add shades of meaning to the chorus each time it repeats. Above all, try to make the events unfold as smoothly as possible. If you find the plot getting sketchy or unclear, you're probably trying to cover too much ground. If you're getting caught up with too much detail, then maybe your tale lacks dramatic moments or a regular flow of new, meaningful information. You might want to make a short outline that states the facts of the event as if it were in a newspaper article before going ahead with the lyric. This can help you organize the facts and pinpoint the important details. The story song is one way that country writers grab the listener's attention. Interesting lyrics can make the simplicity and repetition of country music come alive.

### The Country Vocabulary

Like the blues, country music is most often performed by artists from the South and West, so it naturally contains the colloquialisms and phrasings of the regional dialects. Though country music today seldom contains the ungrammatical "ain'ts" and "yups" of the hillbilly music of yesteryear, you'll probably notice that the final "g" is often dropped in verbs like "lovin' " and "drivin' " and colloquial phrases like "turn me loose" and "bet your bottom dollar" are still the norm. Of course, there's also the CB lingo of the truckers, with "smokies" and "convoys," "burning rubber," and "putting the pedal to the metal." Although the trucking theme has lost popularity in country music, it enjoyed international approval in the 1970s. The dialect and speech patterns used in the typical country song are simply that of the average high-school-educated American working person.

The best way to write natural-sounding country lyrics is to listen to country artists and study their phrasings. You don't need to use actual southernisms in the lyrics. The performer will add them where needed. However, it's very important that you be aware of where they may occur, especially when it comes to crafting your rhymes.

### Imagery

The imagery in country songs is taken from the landscape of country living, from sunsets and meadows to truckstops and barrooms. Many country tunes use images that serve as metaphors for some aspect of the song's message. The

country classic "The Queen of the Silver Dollar" relies on vivid honky-tonk imagery and symbols of royalty to paint its sad portrait of a wasted woman.

> *She's the queen of the Silver Dollar.*
> *She rules this smoky kingdom.*
> *Her scepter is a wine glass,*
> *And this barstool is her throne.*
>
> *And the jesters flock around her*
> *And fight to win her favors*
> *And see which one will take the queen*
> *Of the Silver Dollar home.*

Almost every line contains ironic juxtaposition—an image of royalty combined
with a commonplace image from honky-tonk life. This technique drives home
the paradoxical, touching portrait of a woman who is certainly a big fish in a
little pond.

Don't hesitate to interweave images throughout your lyric. Sometimes a little
detail, like the particular make of a car or the smoke in a barroom, can be just
what's needed to bring a dramatic event into focus.

### Rhyme

Most country performers have a fairly free and colloquial delivery, so, to an
extent, imperfect rhyming seems natural in the country lyric. But these are often
balanced with perfect rhymes and double rhymes. In the lyric of "Crime of Passion" above, imperfect rhymes like "over" and "Nova" or "pains" and "names"
don't break the flow at all. That's because the rhyme scheme is quite strict and
regular, ABABCDCDEFGFG for the verse and ABCABB for the chorus. The first
rhyme we hear is a rare perfect triple—"El Dorado" and "Colorado." And many
more perfect rhymes give the lyric a sense of tightness and polish—"pleat" and
"seat," "job" and "rob," "honey" and "money." "The Queen of the Silver Dollar"
has a less demanding and more traditional pattern—ABCDEFGD. Notice that
the only rhyme in the verse is imperfect: "throne" and "home." The lyricist has
taken care, though, to create partial rhymes at the end of lines five and six with
"around her" and "her favor." In these lyrics, the focus is on the ironic metaphor
and visual imagery rather than a tight rhyme scheme. Chances are that more
rhyming would here make the lyricist's job impossible.

Let your ears be the judge of whether your rhymes sound natural. Remember,
the real goal of your rhyme scheme is to tie the lyric together, not to be obtrusive
or call attention to itself. Double rhyming is a favorite in country lyrics, but don't
try to force it. Contrived rhymes go against the grain of the typical country

message, which requires sincerity and naturalness to make its point. As country songwriter Wesley Rose puts it, "Country songs use the words that Lincoln used."

## Country and Western Music

Since the lyrics are all-important, the melodies of country songs are most often simple, almost conversational. Extensive use is made of the major scale and the outlining of the basic triads of the I, IV, and V chords. Consider this example, similar to the opening of the Bob Wills classic "Faded Love."

Many country songwriters also make use of the major pentatonic scale. This is a five-note scale made up of the root, second, third, fifth, and sixth degrees of a major scale.

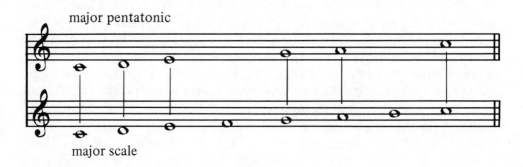

A good example of the major pentatonic is in the first few notes of Pee Wee King's "Tennessee Waltz." A more recent example of both triad outlining and use of the major pentatonic scale is the dramatic opening to the chorus of George Jones's hit "Wine Colored Roses." The entire chorus of this song, save one note, stays within the major pentatonic scale.

notes of triad

Country songs that are influenced by other genres, such as blues, rock, swing, and pop, make use of the melodic devices common to those styles.

The simple, narrative quality of most country lyrics forces most of the melodies into fairly regular forms, with the four- or six-line verse/chorus model being the most common.

### Typical Rhythms

Since early country and western music derived its rhythm from the guitar, many country songs still employ what could be called a "strumming rhythm."

This basic "boom-chicka" rhythm is heard in the early country recordings by the Carter Family, Jimmie Rodgers, Hank Williams, and others. It was featured to great advantage by Johnny Cash's guitarist Luther Perkins in such hits as "I Walk the Line" and "Folsom Prison Blues." Although this particular rhythm has been toned down considerably in today's country songs, it is still the dominant underlying $\frac{4}{4}$ rhythm.

Since western swing evolved as dance music, the *two-step* rhythm was prevalent in addition to the standard swing rhythm (see "Jazz"). The two-step rhythm is a simple, strong $\frac{2}{4}$.

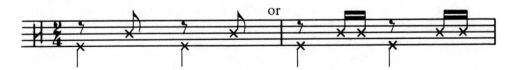

Both country ballads and uptunes also make use of the *shuffle* rhythm (see "Blues"), often supported with equal accents on all four beats.

This rhythm, the strong four pointed up by a walking bass line, is typical of much honky-tonk music.

Country music is unique among popular music genres in its partiality toward the waltz. This is probably because the waltz remained a favorite dance among country fans long after it had ceased to be popular with listeners and dancers favoring other kinds of music. The typical waltz rhythm is a simple $\frac{3}{4}$ with an accent on one.

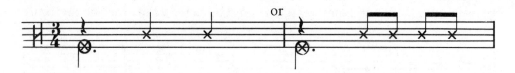

The contemporary country waltz places a prominent accent on three as well as on one. This is usually pointed up by a snare drum crack on the third beat and gives a strong sense of movement quite unlike the traditional dance rhythm.

### Typical Progressions

To understand the elements of good country songwriting, it is essential to listen to the older material of the genre, much more so than with other popular song idioms. This is especially true when it comes to basic harmonic structure. As a rule, a true country song sticks close to one of several classic chord progressions, and so many country songs exhibit very similar harmonic frameworks. This simple, traditional feel to the chord structure is what makes a country song. For instance, there are probably hundreds of country songs that share the following sixteen-bar progression; three that come to mind are the traditional "Great Speckled Bird," Hank Williams's "Your Cheatin' Heart," and the Willie Nelson/Waylon Jennings hit "Luckenbach, Texas."

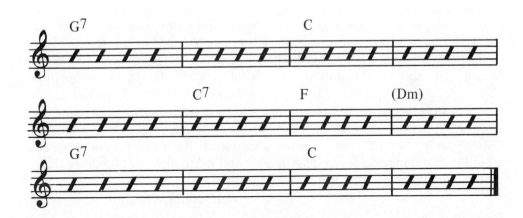

Two typically country harmonic devices are the use of the V of V and the IV of IV. These are commonly employed when either the V or IV chord is held for a measure or two as an embellishment to a simple chord progression. Here is the beginning of a model country chord progression, first straight, then with an added IV of IV and V of V:

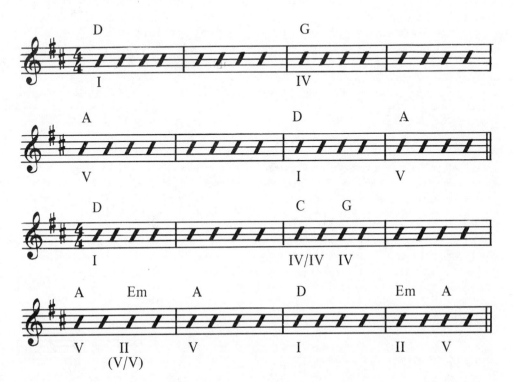

In the example above, the V of V is a diatonic II minor chord; you could also use an E7 in its place, which would be the true V chord of the A.

The chord progressions in country ballads may be jazz-influenced, like Willie Nelson's "Crazy" and "Nightlife," or pop-influenced, like Kris Kristofferson's "Help Me Make It Through the Night" or Harlan Howard's "I Fall to Pieces." Country uptunes tend to favor more rock-influenced harmonies, like Dave Dudley's "Six Days on the Road" or the Judds's "Girls' Night Out." There are also typically country types of progressions for ballads and uptunes that are rooted in the honky-tonk, western swing, and fiddle-tune or bluegrass traditions, or in a combination of these traditions.

The most important thing to remember when writing a country song is that no matter how it is influenced by another type of music, there must always be some strong element of the country tradition in there somewhere. This is true of music and lyrics, and it makes the difference between a song's being accepted as country or its being classed as imitation or unconvincing.

# 13

# *Rock and Roll*

*All we did was take country music and give it a colored beat.*

—Carl Perkins

*I heard the tenor saxophones of Red Prysock and Big Al Sears. I heard the blues-singing, piano-playing Ivory Joe Hunter. I wondered. I wondered for about a week. Then I went to the station manager and I talked him into permitting me to follow my programme with a rock 'n' roll party.*

—Alan Freed

## Rockabilly and the Birth of Rock and Roll

When rock and roll emerged in the 1950s, it caught on like wildfire. The exciting sound of black R&B artists already had a sturdy following when white country performers like Carl Perkins and Bill Haley reinterpreted traditional country and western music with an R&B beat. Because of its "hillbilly" roots, a lot of early rock and roll is termed "rockabilly," a name that stuck for a few years, but was more or less dropped by 1960. The typical rockabilly song was designed to feature a raw-edged vocal in the style of the black blues shouters of the forties and fifties. Rockabilly music was characterized by a fast $\frac{4}{4}$ shuffle rhythm. The driving "rock" beat was usually carried by a walking bass line and accented with a sparse rhythm guitar part. Rockabilly tunes also usually featured a blistering electric guitar solo, a trademark of the rock and roll style to this day.

Though mainstream rock and roll moved quickly away from its country roots, rockabilly continued to exert its influence on progressive country music of the sixties and seventies. In fact, some of today's legendary country artists, including George Jones, Conway Twitty, and Johnny Cash, were among the biggest rock and roll stars of the fifties. So it makes sense that rockabilly's echoes may still be heard in the mainstream country music of the present day.

### Rock Comes into Its Own

Bill Haley's "Rock Around the Clock" went to the number one position on the pop charts in 1955 and is often credited as being the first true rock and roll song. That same year, Chuck Berry released "Maybellene," and Elvis Presley had eleven chart hits, including "Heartbreak Hotel" and "Blue Suede Shoes." Rockabilly was no longer a novelty music, but it had entered the pop mainstream, and was now known as rock and roll.

It is generally accepted that the name "rock and roll" was first coined by disc jockey Alan Freed in 1954 for his popular radio broadcast, "The Rock and Roll Show." What was considered rock and roll at this time was essentially the rockabilly and progressive rhythm and blues of both white and black artists.

Most of the star writers and performers of this period were based in the southern states from Texas to Tennessee, as well as in the major urban centers across the country: Philadelphia, New York, Chicago, Detroit, and Los Angeles. Some of the more influential recordings of the mid-fifties came out of Memphis, Tennesee, recorded by Sam Phillips at Sun Records. Sun put out the early recordings of Carl Perkins, Jerry Lee Lewis, Johnny Cash, and, of course, Elvis Presley. The overwhelming response of European and American teenagers to the music of artists such as Jerry Lee Lewis, Chuck Berry, Little Richard, and Elvis Presley made the world aware of rock and roll.

### The British Invasion

By the early sixties, rock and roll seemed to be getting fragmented from its attempts at making it big on the pop charts. Many recordings by pop artists featured watered-down elements of rock, and even Elvis Presley didn't sound like he had in 1956. Contending with the smooth sounds of surfing music and the controversial themes and attitudes being expressed in song by members of the folk/protest movement, rock seemed in danger of being absorbed into the mainstream of pop music as just another influential fad, a fate that doomsayers had been predicting for rock and roll since 1955.

But then, in 1964, the Beatles came along with a strong new rock energy and hip performance style that brought the rock craze to a frenzy. Other British rock groups, like the Rolling Stones, the Dave Clark Five, and the Who, followed suit and gave rock and roll an English accent. British rockers like David Bowie and Elvis Costello still have a strong influence on the changing shape of rock today.

Curiously enough, the influential British groups like the Beatles and the Rolling Stones drew their inspiration directly from rockabilly and rhythm and blues. But their reinterpretations of the original rock sound spurred new developments by American artists rather than simply perpetuating the older styles. Their initial popularity also created a demand for almost any kind of British pop music resulting in the success of artists like Herman's Hermits, Freddie and the Dreamers, Chad and Jeremy, and Peter and Gordon, all of whom had little to do with rock music. As certain American bands tried to copy or counter the British sound, more pop influence crept into rock. Combined with such other influences, as the music of folk-rock artists like Bob Dylan and Donovan, this trend led to the advent of soft rock and pop-rock.

### Rock and Roll Today

Rock and roll is the predominant musical style on the pop charts today. However, over the years, it has become more and more difficult to categorize rock as a single distinct style: this problem has given rise to such terms as acid rock, soft rock, pop-rock, glitter rock, southern rock, artrock, hardcore, and heavy metal. Perhaps the best general definition of rock today is any popular music with a simple, driving beat and a small-band instrumentation that features guitar and vocals.

## Rock Themes

To identify their new music, the rock songwriters of the fifties often focused their themes on the rhythm and music of rock itself. Rock-inspired dance crazes also naturally provided rich theme material for the songs of this period. The other popular theme of rock and roll lyrics is the mainstay of all popular musics: love and romance.

A reexamination of authority and the cornerstone institutions in America occurred among young people in the late fifties and sixties. Rock and roll music has long been identified as a unifying force in this phase of American cultural development. During the sixties, rock lyrics often reflected on the sociopolitical aspects of American life, particularly in light of the Vietnam war, the Civil Rights Movement, the drug culture, and various other controversies involving human freedoms and class distinctions. Rock and roll became a mouthpiece for these social concerns through the work of the more outspoken artists of the day, including Bob Dylan, the Beatles, and the Rolling Stones. Although the sociopolitical themes in rock songs of the eighties are perhaps not as heated and multivarious as those of the sixties, there are still vestiges of these concerns in today's rock message. This is particularly true of the themes of today's heavy metal and punk songs that are directed toward the younger listener. Feelings of rebellion toward family members, school, and employers are expressed in the work of such artists as Black Sabbath, Pink Floyd, and Billy Idol.

Like most popular music, rock and roll has had its share of songs that deal with novelty or fantasy themes, abundant in the work of such artists as the Beatles, Jethro Tull, and David Bowie. Imaginative and whimsical lyrics have always worked well in the evocative and free-form rock setting. Metaphorical journeys and revelations are superb vehicles for the rock songwriter who wishes to do some consciousness-raising in an entertaining way.

## The Rock and Roll Title

Self-referential rock titles have been popular from the very first, with Bill Haley's milestone hit, "Rock Around the Clock." Many more songwriters and lyricists followed suit with such tunes as Presley's 1957 "Jailhouse Rock," Chuck Berry's 1957 "Rock and Roll Music," and Guy Mitchell's 1957 "Rock-A-Billy." Some pop songwriters joined the bandwagon with such hits as "Rock and Roll Waltz" recorded by Kay Starr in 1956, a teenager's amusing and even touching account of her parents' attempt to waltz to a rock and roll tune. Rock music itself is still a popular theme for the title of the eighties, as in Def Leppard's "Rock of Ages" and "I Love Rock 'n' Roll," by Joan Jett and the Blackhearts.

Part of the reason for rock and roll's booming success was the many dance crazes it inspired throughout the fifties and sixties, like the twist, the monkey, the watusi, and the swim. Thus, many of the first rock tunes allude to dancing and the social dance scene—Danny and the Juniors' "At the Hop" of 1958 and Chubby Checker's "The Twist" of 1960 (which also held the number one position in its 1962 revival). Rock and roll– and disco-influenced dancing are still very popular today, as reflected in such titles as David Bowie's pop-rock hit "Let's Dance" and Lionel Richie's "Dancing on the Ceiling."

Titles that express themes of love and romance, and their inherent difficulties are the stock-in-trade of rock and roll. Chicago's "Will You Still Love Me?" and Bon Jovi's "You Give Love a Bad Name" are typical of the straightforward approach that works best. Where love and rock and roll are concerned, it rarely pays to be too clever or complex. This is not to say that you should aim for one-dimensional treatments of this theme, but rather accept the interesting challenge of expressing it in a fresh and captivating way. Sensuality and sexuality have become more and more frankly expressed in rock and roll titles, ranging from the frank yet coy approach of Robert Palmer's "I Didn't Mean to Turn You On," to George Michael's frontal "I Want Your Sex." Don't get too carried away with sexual allusions and erotic images in your rock themes and titles. Remember, the more controversial your material, the more your work will be limited to only the most open-minded listeners and artists.

Sociopolitical themes inspired many rock titles of the 1960s and 1970s. Although social issues are still treated in today's rock songs, the message of protest and rebellion against the establishment has softened with the times. Janis Ian's 1967 rock ballad "Society's Child (Baby I've Been Thinking)" is a dramatic portrait of an interracial teenage relationship that is shattered by social disapproval. Today, Stevie Wonder and Paul McCartney are much more matter of fact in their treatment of a similar theme in "Ebony and Ivory," in which the keys of the piano serve as an elegant metaphor for interracial love and cooperation.

Novelty and fantasy themes are still popular with today's rock songwriter. Titles like the Bangles's "Walk Like an Egyptian," the Moody Blues's "Your Wildest Dreams," and Genesis's "Invisible Touch" are just a few of the many imaginative themes permissible. If you use a title like this for your song, be sure that the meaning of the image is fully explained by the end of the song. If the image leaves the listener with a cryptic message, the meaning of your song will be forgotten. If you take the listener on a meaningful journey or portray a novel image in an interesting way, you can be pretty sure your song will be remembered.

## Rock Lyrics

A good rock song should never beat around the bush. The minute the lyric starts to ramble, the essential movement that is so much a part of the rock and roll sound is lost. A strong and repetitive song form is always at the root of a lyric that moves and conveys the message succinctly, with memorable images and bold strokes. Though its themes may range from brief personal encounters to outcries for world peace, rock and roll has a down-to-earth and frank quality that makes it able to cross cultural barriers with its vivifying message of optimism and excitement.

Like its relatives—rhythm and blues, disco, and funk—rock and roll has always professed its own power to stimulate the listener's emotional response. Many people even feel that rock and roll has a unique therapeutic quality: the listener transcends any of his or her own feelings of repression or stagnation by surrendering to the insistent pulse of the music. Many young people also turn to rock and roll as a way of fortifying their sense of identity and group belonging. The musical style respresents modern culture itself in its most progressive and fun-loving aspect. Most rock and roll lyrics today are written in this spirit.

Many rock lyrics focus on the evocative effects of music as it relates to the growth and change of human identity and the ability to love and be loved. The Psychedelic Furs' recent success "Heartbreak Beat" describes rock and roll's ability to inspire feelings of romance in listeners: "There's a heartbreak beat and it feels like love." This song is a perfect example of a rock song that focuses on its own powerful effects. There's mention made of the humanizing power of dancing with "nobody don't dance on the edge of the dark," and the image of an attentive rock listener who's "got the radio on." This just goes to show that it can't hurt to incorporate references to rock and roll's ability to evoke an emotional response from, and even between, its own listeners.

Meat Loaf portrays a very different view of rock and roll music in his "Rock 'N' Roll Mercenaries," a commentary on the insincere and commercial aspects of some of today's rock and roll. The lyric portrays the creators of this low-grade music as "soldiers of fortune" who will produce "anything you pay to hear." The kernel of his complaint is that this type of rock and roll is produced "not for the song" or "for the love," but to satisy its creators' insatiable desire for commercial profits. Although it is difficult to picture Meat Loaf as the Ralph Nader of rock and roll, he has a point about some of the slap-dash, hyped-up rock that seems to make trend-seekers so willing to part with their money. Meat Loaf's judgmental view of his own chosen style would not have as much power in the mouth of a lesser-known artist or songwriter. Certain themes require an artistic reputation to back them up.

It's important that rock lyrics express a certain broad-minded outlook or hipness, a tone that is often developed through phrasing and choice of language. As you are working on your own lyrics, it helps to develop your themes in the most bare-bones and direct way possible. If an image or detail seems difficult to fit in or to develop, chances are it doesn't belong in the song. Don't be afraid to cut off the fat and deal with the heart of the matter. Although *non sequiturs* and hazy imagery are observable in quite a few of today's successful rock lyrics, it isn't a good idea to emulate those songs that generate the listener's interest with a hyped-up rap. This is the brand of rock and roll that will be most quickly forgotten with the years, while the more meaningful rock songs live on.

### The Vocabulary of Rock

As we have said, word choice can do a lot to make a rock lyric sound natural and hip. The most important guideline is that wordiness and complicated phrasing can really throw a wrench into the gears. If a word or phrase calls too much attention to itself, or if it doesn't flow along as freely and easily as the music, then it simply doesn't work.

Rock still shows the influence of blues and country music. Thus, rock lyrics generally contain informal spellings and phrasings like "rockin' " for "rocking" and "wanna" for "want to." Rock and roll doesn't have a slang of its own. If a slang word is commonly used in conversations you hear, then it is appropriate in the rock setting. Thus, current expressions like "you look excellent" are perfectly appropriate to describe an attractive character. Let your common sense and your knowledge of the type of people who listen to rock and roll be your guide when it comes to developing your own rock vocabulary.

## Imagery

Imagery is very important in rock lyrics, especially when plain words can't convey the emotional and direct quality of your message. Metaphor has always been a favored tool of the rock lyricist to provide a strong link between idea and image. Lone Justice's recent success "Shelter" is just one example that relies on imagery to illustrate the song's main theme. The speaker asks to serve as a metaphorical "shelter" for a loved one who is buffeted by the trials of life and loneliness, as depicted by an image of the "storm outside." The songwriters reiterate this theme in a verse with a striking set of related images:

> *Disillusion*
> *Has an edge so sharp*
> *It tears at your soul*
> *And leaves a stain upon your heart*
> *I need you*
> *To wash mine clean*
> *You felt it too*
> *And you need me.*

The profound theme of spiritual death and purification through love would be seem thin or flip were it not couched in the metaphor of the knife and the characters' wounded hearts. By carrying through with these images as they relate to the song's thematic love relationship, the writers have created emotional intensity, meaning, and visual interest with a carefully constructed set of metaphorical images. This is one of the best techniques for adding depth and meaning to a song's lyric, without sounding preachy or clichéd.

## Rhyme

Although the typical rock lyric will permit a liberal use of imperfect rhymes, it is important to put true rhymes in key positions of the song to fortify its form and thus accentuate its overall sense of power and movement. As a general rule, have a strong perfect rhyme in the final line of each verse and chorus section, although a close imperfect rhyme like "takes" and "brake" or "layer" and "stare" is also acceptable. It pays to place the song's hook line in a strong rhyming position, or to reinforce it with rhymes in repetition. Although double rhymes like "maybe" and "baby" were popular in the rock and roll of the fifties and sixties, they tend to sound stilted in today's rock lyric unless they are carefully chosen for their inherent naturalness and meaning.

As you are building your own rhyme schemes, remember that your main objective is to reinforce the musical and lyrical pattern of each section of the song. If you find that it is not possible to come up with a rhyme that provides for a simple and direct statement of your message, it's better to alter the existing line than to twist another. As a general rule, keep your rhyme schemes as simple and direct as the lyric itself. Plain rhymes go a lot further in rock songs than rhymes that sound clever or poetic.

## The Music of Rock

Rock music's detractors often point out its scarcity of melodic and harmonic invention. In a way they are right: rock melodies and chord progressions are usually simplistic and are subordinate to the all-important beat. But if you really understand and appreciate rock, you know that this is not a shortcoming, but rather rock's strength. After all, the rock and roll beat is what distinguished the form in the first place. The structures, harmonies, and melodies were for the most part simply adapted from those of blues, country, and jazz.

### Rock Melody

Many of the classic rock and roll songs of the fifties are very directly related to the blues. They make use of the standard twelve-bar blues format with its prescribed melodic repetitions. Songs like Chuck Berry's "Johnny B. Goode," "Speedo," by the Cadillacs and Lieber and Stoller's "Hound Dog," recorded by Big Mama Thornton and Elvis Presley are nothing more than blues songs set to the new rock and roll beat. The melody of "Rock Around the Clock" also displays the typical country melodic device of outlining triads.

This melody, like many others of its era, contains a liberal sprinkling of *blue notes* (flatted thirds and sevenths) throughout the song.

A lot of rock songwriters today still make use of the blues scale. This is a good way to evoke a fifties sound, if used in a calculated, lighthearted way, as in "Rock Around the Clock" or a tough, earthy rock mood, as in Cream's "Sunshine of Your Love." Straight major and minor scales can be used to good effect, too: consider the raunchy Rolling Stones classic "Honky Tonk Women," the melody of which lies entirely within the major scale.

Many of today's rock melodies also borrow ideas freely from jazz and pop as well as from Latin, reggae, and black music. Heavy metal songs in particular make use of some of the modal and altered scales common in jazz. Various rock and pop-rock artists (like the Police and Paul Simon, for example) have assimilated the clipped melodic phrases and repetitive motifs of reggae and African music.

### Typical Rock Progressions

Early rock and roll also lifted its chord progressions from the standard twelve-bar blues form. Songs like "Blue Suede Shoes," "Tutti-Frutti," and "Hound Dog" adhere strictly to this form. After its first burst of energy, rock and roll began to assimilate other influences and develop new forms. One of these was the rock ballad, which most often used some variation on this standard progression:

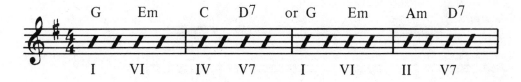

This progression was often used for the A section of a standard AABA format with a bridge starting on the IV chord, as in "In the Still of the Night," "Silhouettes," and "Dream." This type of progression is usually used to evoke the fifties era of rock, as in Billy Joel's "The Longest Time" and Ronnie Milsap's "Lost in the Fifties Tonight."

Much of the best rock is what is affectionately known as "three-chord rock". The three chords are of course usually I, IV, and V. These three form the basis of rock songs as diverse as "I Wanna Be Sedated," "Glory Days," and "You Can Call Me Al." Other common sets of three chords are I, IV, and flat-VII (IV of IV), which shows up in songs like "My Generation," "Dirty Water," and "Get Back;" and I, flat-VI, and flat-VII, immortalized in "Old Man Down the Road."

*Rock Rhythms*

The earliest rock beat was a strong $\frac{4}{4}$ with heavy backbeats on two and four, a rhythm developed naturally from the practice of "slapping" the upright bass common in the early rock ensembles. At this point, the melodic rhythms and phrase lengths were almost universally appropriated from the twelve-bar blues songs of earlier days. Good examples would be Little Richard's "Tutti Frutti" and Jerry Lee Lewis's "Great Balls of Fire."

Toward the end of the fifties, the music had begun to develop some rhythmic sophistication. While the speeded-up blues formats were still the underlying model for rock songs, artists from Buddy Holly, with "Peggy Sue" and "Not Fade Away," to Fats Domino, with "I'm Walkin' " and "Blueberry Hill," were demonstrating the form's rhythmic adaptability. Also at this time the prototypical rock and roll ballad emerged, employing the slow $\frac{6}{4}$ with a backbeat on four. This rhythm, long a mainstay of blues, has today found its way via rock into country and soul songs.

Both of these seminal rhythms are still very much around and underpinning many rock songs. In addition, rock songs may make use of typical disco, country, reggae, and funk rhythms in both their melodic and underlying rhythms. Here are a few of these types of rhythms in outline. Tap them out, play them on your instrument, or program them into a sequencer or drum machine to get the feel. After all, a lot of rock songs start out with nothing more than "the beat."

Disco

Country

Reggae

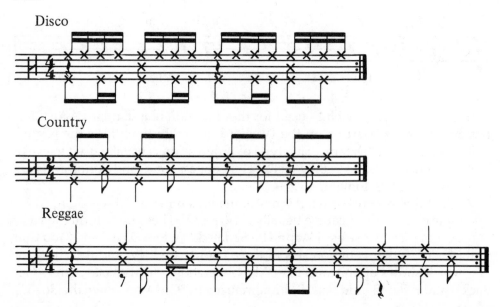

Funk

Though there are many styles and flavors of rock-influenced popular music today, they all capitalize on the listener's own sense of rhythm and movement. It is important that these qualities of rock music are expressed as a natural outgrowth of the human experience. The songwriter's work and the performer's delivery should work together to create a frank picture of human emotion and evoke the listener's sympathetic response. But the only way to write meaningful and lasting rock and roll music and lyrics is to stick to ideas that mean something to you, and tell it like it is.

# 14

# *Pop*

*There've been several revolutions that have taken place in pop music since I started writing, and I think they were all improvements.*

*—Gerry Goffin*

*A while ago I was worried about slipping out of the mainstream, or any stream, so I decided to write a song for Tom Jones. I didn't give him the song, but I did write it. It was a fairly representative Tom Jones song, not a good one, just a representative one. It made me feel pretty good for a while.*

*—Randy Newman*

*Pop music can include any form of music that captures the public fancy, from dreamy instrumentals to barking dogs. . . .*

*—Joel Whitburn*

## The History of Pop

The history of pop music of the last three decades involves a variety of performers of diverse musical backgrounds and styles from Mitch Miller, Mario Lanza, and Doris Day to Boy George, Jim Croce, and Aretha Franklin. Even today, pop ranges from the true rock sound of Bruce Springsteen to the disco-influenced style of Madonna. The term "pop" has always been used to refer to the music of a given period that is most popular among music listeners.

### The Popular Music of Yesteryear

Folk music relies on oral tradition for its dissemination and growth; in other words, it is passed along from person to person only through performance. The term "popular music" implies the presence of a music industry promoting in the form of published sheet music, recordings, or paid performances. In 1800, there were several professional music publishers in Philadelphia and by 1820, there were publishers in southern cities as well. Most of the music produced at this time was of English and Irish origin. It was not until the 1830s that American songwriters began to achieve international success. One of the main venues for popular song at this time was the traveling minstrel show. Many minstrel songs were the Euro-American songwriter's reflection of the black folk music of the day and they were sung by blackface performers. In the 1840s, Stephen Foster combined the best parts of the Euro-American and black American folk traditions and created hundreds of songs like "Camptown Races" and "The Old Folks at Home." As the United States' first internationally renowned songwriter, Stephen Foster is, in effect, the father of American popular song.

### Tin Pan Alley and Vaudeville

The music industry flourished in the last half of the nineteenth century, largely through the sale of sheet music, pianos, and organs. Many of the most successful songs of this period were created for, or drawn from, the repertoire of the minstrel show. Publishers still relied on performers to "plug" their latest songs and this relationship grew even stronger as the minstrel tradition blossomed into American vaudeville.

The typical vaudeville show featured a variety of different entertainers, from opera singers, soft-shoe dancers, and comedy teams to contortionists and animal acts. Vaudeville theaters sprang up in cities all over the country to accommodate the public's growing interest in this form of entertainment. With its many theaters, barrooms, and dancehalls, New York City was a busy center of American vaudeville. The vaudeville district stretched between West 14th and 30th streets in New York City, where many theaters and clubs attracted a sizable vaudeville audience.

By 1890, several music publishers had also located here, particularly on West 26th, 27th, and 28th Streets, an area that became popularly known as Tin Pan Alley. Most scholars agree that this name came from the collective din of piano music that emanated from the windows of the music companies that lined the street. As the theater district moved further uptown to the Broadway area we know today, the music publishers also relocated to be near the singing stars and the songwriters of the stage. Eventually, the term Tin Pan Alley came to mean the whole of the American popular music industry of the first part of this century.

In 1893, Charles K. Harris's "After the Ball" became the first popular song to sell a million copies and by 1903, over ten million copies of the sheet music had been sold. The gay nineties and early 1900s saw the heyday of the sentimental

Victorian ballad and clever novelty number. Sentimental ballads like "In the Shade of the Old Apple Tree" and "Little Annie Rooney" were the biggest sellers during this period. Also popular were comic songs like George M. Cohan's "So Long Mary" from the musical play *Forty-five Minutes from Broadway*. The sugary Victorian ballad fell from popularity twenty years later with the advent of the recording industry, and the birth of commercial jazz and blues. Now Tin Pan Alley drew on a variety of new sources, from black artists to "hillbilly" yodelers. Still, the main source of popular music in America from 1900 up until the late 1940s was the Broadway stage, which yielded many hit songs by such great writers as George and Ira Gershwin, Jerome Kern, Richard Rodgers, Oscar Hammerstein II, Lorenz Hart, and Harold Arlen.

## The Diversity of Pop

Early American popular music and popular music today cannot really be characterized as a particular style of music, but rather as a blend of the chosen styles of the times. However, during the fifties, pop music did emerge as a distinctive musical style, typified by the work of artists like Bing Crosby, Frank Sinatra, Perry Como, Doris Day, and Andy Williams. Many people use the term pop to refer to the music which was characterized by lilting melodies and pleasant harmonies, usually featured in big band or orchestral arrangements with vocal backgrounds.

When rock and roll burst on the scene in the mid-fifties, nobody was really sure how long it was going to last. But it sure was popular, and this era saw hit songs by Mitch Miller and Dean Martin sharing the charts with those of Elvis Presley and Bill Haley and the Comets. There were also new kinds of music being heard that used elements of rock but sounded a lot different from the rockabilly music that first made it popular. These included the distinctive doo-wop sound popularized by groups like the Marcels and the Five Satins; the girl groups, such as the Shirelles and the Supremes; and surfing music by such groups as the Beach Boys and Jan and Dean. By the time the Beatles arrived in 1964, rock and roll songs had all but completely taken over *Billboard's* "Hot 100" chart.

Throughout the late sixties and early seventies, pop continued to diversify. Subgenres came and went, but always with some lasting influence. The folk boom started the careers of such artists as Bob Dylan, John Denver, and Peter, Paul, and Mary, who, as they drifted toward rock, contributed to the groundwork for the pop-rock and soft rock sounds of artists like Glen Campbell, the Carpenters, and the Eagles. In the eighties, the term pop music is still not much more than a measuring stick of a song's commercial success, but it is generally used to refer to music in the soft rock style, characterized by smooth harmonies and bright vocals.

Today, most pop uptunes are designed to be danceable. The advent of music video has also caused pop music to be suggestive of rich visual images with a strong sense of personality and environment. The hits of mega-stars like Prince, Madonna, and Boy George are representative of today's pop-rock sound, which combines the clear and harmonious qualities of pop music with the hip themes and exciting beat of rock.

## Common Themes

Though pop today is a blend of different musical styles, pop lyrics have always expressed a common or sentimental view of human love, grief, or joy. Normally these themes are presented from the perspective of people in everyday settings. Since the average pop listener is in the age range of early teens to young adult, it's a good idea to veer away from old-fashioned values of overt conservatism and traditional family life.

Pop themes vary from real life romances to fantasy adventures, from dancing and partying to facing up to love's difficult lessons. The emergence of the youth culture of the sixties that fostered the rock and roll movement also injected pop themes with a harder edge. Sexual and socially charged issues are still treated in pop songs today, particularly those that show a strong rock influence. George Michael's "I Want Your Sex" and Madonna's "Like a Virgin" express some of the spicier pop themes that are now permissible.

As you are coming up with your own pop material, keep in mind that most pop music today expresses themes well imbued with romance, love, and sex—or the lack thereof. But you shouldn't think of it as being limited to just one tired-out subject. The real trick is to find an interesting or personal way to express this age-old theme in a fresh way. Sincerity on the part of the songwriter goes a long way.

## The Pop Title

Since love is the most common pop theme of all, many titles say it straight out, as in Tina Turner's "What's Love Got to Do with It" and "Love Power" by Dionne Warwick and Jeffrey Osborne. The difficulties of romance and lost love are also commonly used in titles, such as Chicago's "If She Would Have Been Faithful" or Yes's "Owner of a Lonely Heart." Friendship, too, is popular title material, as in the revivals of "Stand by Me" and "Lean on Me." Since so many pop titles deal with these themes, the list of examples is virtually endless.

Because so much of pop music today is really rock or rock-influenced, many pop songs identify this fact in their titles, as in the Whispers' "Rock Steady" or Billy Joel's "It's Still Rock and Roll to Me." Often a pop title will allude to its own groove or rhythm, and this is especially true of pop-funk—"Rhythm Is Gonna Get You," as recorded by Gloria Estefan and the Miami Sound Machine or the System's "Don't Disturb This Groove." Some titles actually refer to the musicians or vocalist: "Jam Tonight" as recorded by Freddie Jackson, or Kenny G's "Songbird." Since danceability is the main thrust of pop music today, we get titles like Whitney Houston's "I Wanna Dance with Somebody (Who Loves Me)" and David Bowie's "Let's Dance." Some pop tunes also serve as theme songs for movies, and their titles often reiterate the movie title: "Fame," "Footloose," and "Flashdance . . . What a Feeling." Notice that most of these titles reflect a feeling of movement and change.

## Pop Lyrics

Today's pop music bears the influence of many different musical and lyrical styles. With so much variety on the current pop charts, it is difficult to discuss typical pop lyrics. For a detailed discussion of the lyrics of the particular styles that dominate the pop market today, refer to the "Rock" chapter and the sections on rhythm and blues, soul, gospel, funk, and disco in "The Black Sound—From Rhythm and Blues to Rap."

The pop music of the sixties and seventies was characterized by a more distinctive musical and lyrical style. The typically bright harmonies and sweet melodies complemented the lyric's powerful sense of romance and innocence. Pop lyrics often expressed their theme in idealized terms, and the imagery often expressed the idea that, as Ray Stevens put it, "Everything is beautiful in its own way" (an important concept in the movement for aesthetic reevaluation in the 1960s). Even painful breakups and loneliness were often expressed in idealized terms.

Many of the lyrics of pop's heyday would not wash in the popular market today. Innocence and sentimentality have given way to a more realistic view of the world, particularly where romance is concerned. You will find it helpful to study the pop lyrics of yesterday and today, and to analyze them to see what makes them tick.

## Pop Music

Since the pop repertory is generally made up of songs from all genres (i.e., whatever is popular), the musical elements of pop are equally disparate. Most crossover pop hits tend to be ballads from the country, black, and rock charts, as the uptunes of these styles are generally too idiomatic to be considered pop.

Today's standard pop ballad (if there is such a thing) would have to be the power ballad, typified by such songs as "Endless Love" and "That's What Friends Are For." As stated elsewhere, the power ballad stresses held notes at the upper end of the song's range. Think of "I know I'll never love this way again." These dramatic melodies usually make use of the major scale and feature the techniques of simply repeating and sequencing motifs and phrases. A good example is Leo Sayer's number one pop hit "When I Need You," which employs an obvious downward sequence at the beginning of the verse as well as other types of motivic repetition throughout.

The chord progressions of pop hits are drawn from all genres but most often conform to those of what has come to be called "soft rock." Soft rock progressions are usually slightly jazz-influenced in that they may make use of Major Seventh, Major Sixth, Ninth, and other "jazz chords." Masters of this music include the Eagles, the Doobie Brothers, and Billy Joel.

A strong beat is a mainstay of the pop song, even though the underlying rhythms are usually not as driving or insistent as those of rock or soul songs. A common rhythm in contemporary pop makes good use of the traditional backbeat rhythm common in blues, rock, and country songs.

This pattern can be very effective on slow tunes ("Best of My Love," "The Morning After" ) where the snare drum crack on three may be accented to quite a degree. If you have this kind of accompaniment in mind while writing the tune, make sure that the melody leaves some breathing space around the third beat in every measure. With less prominent accenting, the pattern also shows up in many pop uptunes ("I Say a Little Prayer," "Go Your Own Way").

Pop songs influenced by rock, jazz, country, and soul adhere to the musical conventions of those styles. The ballad forms of these genres are ready material for crossover to pop; the uptunes are usually slightly softened compared to the true classics of each respective genre. However, this is not always the case, and a really great song with a far-reaching theme may top several charts.

# *Appendices*

## Copyright Basics

If copyright laws did not exist in the United States today, songwriters would have no protection against unrestricted and uncompensated use of their property. In theory, the law is quite simple: when you create an original song, you own the copyright. As the copyright owner of a song, you have certain exclusive rights, which you may exercise.

- The right to reproduce the copyrighted work in copies or phonorecords.
- The right to prepare derivative works based upon the copyrighted work.
- The right to distribute copies or phonorecords of the copyrighted work to the public by sale or other transfer of ownership, or by rental, lease, or lending.
- The right to perform the copyrighted work publicly.
- The right to display the copyrighted work publicly.

With one exception, what these rights mean is that if anyone else wants to do any of these things, they must obtain your permission. The one exception is the first one listed. Once your song has been recorded and commercially distributed, anyone may record it as long as they pay you the compulsory license fee (5 cents per selection per record or tape for up to 5 minutes of playing time. Anything over 5 minutes starts at .95 cents per minute of playing time.) The law grants you these rights for life plus fifty years.

### Registering a Song for Copyright

Many people confuse registering a song for copyright with copyrighting a song. Since the law gives you the copyright to your song from the moment you create it, you don't have to do anything to copyright your work. Registering a song with the Copyright Office of the Library of Congress in Washington, D.C., simply provides proof that you wrote it and when.

However, the only sure way to protect an unpublished work is to register it with the Copyright Office. You may have heard of the so-called "poor man's" copyright. This involves sending a copy of your song to yourself in a registered letter. The idea is that if you can prove that you never opened the envelope, you have proof from the government that the song existed in a fixed form on a certain date. Although this form of proof has stood up in court, sometimes it has not. What you should do is to file form PA with the United States government. The government will send you this form if you write to them at this address:

> United States Copyright Office
> Library of Congress
> Washington, DC 20559
> 202/287-9100

The form is quite easy to fill out, and on it you can register one song or a whole bunch of songs as a "songbook." (The latter method saves money, as you must pay a fee of $10 for every form submitted.) You send in the form, along with two copies of your song, either leadsheets or tape recordings, and within a few months the Copyright Office will send you a certificate of registration.

There are many misconceptions about copyright and copyright infringement. Here are just a few facts that are often misunderstood:

- There is no specified number of notes or measures that you can legally steal from a copyrighted tune. Lawsuits have been won on three notes and lost on eight measures. If you have written a song that is very reminiscent of another classic song, be wary (think of George Harrison and "My Sweet Lord" ["He's So Fine"]).
- You cannot copyright just a title or a chord progression. In order to be considered an original work, your song must have a melody and rhythm. However, the title and chord progression are protected as part of the song.
- You cannot copyright a concept for a song. If this were possible, there would be only one song about dancing and only one about falling in love.
- The act of registering a song with the Office of Copyright does not constitute proof of a valid claim to copyright. When the Office of Copyright registers your song, all they are doing is putting it on file. They do not run a search to make sure that the song does not infringe on the copyright of an existing work.

There is a lot more to know about copyright, and if you are determined to make songwriting your business, you should seek the services of a reputable entertainment lawyer to advise you on matters such as setting up your own publishing company, keeping proper records, and protecting your work in general.

## Commercial and Professional Organizations

### Performing Rights Organizations

Performing rights organizations look out for the welfare of their members by collecting and distributing royalties that come from live performances, and radio, television, juke box, synchronization (film), and other types of playings. In addition, the three organizations listed below provide a host of educational seminars and programs for both the tyro and the experienced songwriter.

> ASCAP
> (American Society of Composers, Authors, and Publishers)
> One Lincoln Plaza
> New York, New York  10019
> 212/595-3050
>
> BMI
> (Broadcast Music Inc.)
> 320 West 57 Street
> New York, New York  10019
> 212/586-2000
>
> SESAC, Inc.
> (Selected Editions of Standard American Catalogues [formerly, the Society of European Stage Authors and Composers])
> 10 Columbus Circle
> New York, New York  10019
> 212/586-1708

### Other Music Associations

American Composers Alliance
170 W. 74 Street
New York, New York
10023
ACA's membership is largely made up of composers of serious music. ACA distributes members' unpublished works to music dealers, music schools, and other academic institutions—and helps to arrange and subsidize recordings and broadcasts of their music.

Black Music Association
1500 Locust Street
Philadelphia, Pennsylvania
19102
This is an organization devoted to the advancement, enrichment, and recognition of black music.

The Dramatists Guild, Inc.
234 West 44 Street
New York, New York  10036
212/398-9366

This is an association for playwrights, composers, and lyricists. It provides contract and other legal counseling, an annual marketing directory, symposiums, workshops, field trips, and an excellent publication, *The Dramatists Guild Quarterly.*

NSAI
(Nashville Songwriters Association, International)
803 Eighteenth Avenue South
Nashville, Tennessee  37203
615/321-5004

With forty locations on the East Coast, this organization is an important one for songwriters. It is dedicated to advancing the profession of songwriting and conducts many educational seminars.

The Songwriters Guild (formerly, the American Guild of Authors of Authors and Composers [AGAC])
276 Fifth Avenue
New York, New York  10001
212/686-6820

The Guild performs services similar to the performing rights societies listed above.

## Unions

AF of M
(American Federation of Musicians)
1500 Broadway
New York, New York  10036

The AF of M is the union that represents musicians, arrangers, contractors, and copyists. It determines the minimum union wage allowable for the employment of its members and provides health insurance and a pension fund to members as well. This organization also maintains certain codes regarding the nature and schedule of members' work to guard against overlong hours or otherwise improper work environments.

AFTRA
(American Federation of Television and Radio Artists)
1350 Avenue of the Americas
New York, New York  10019

AFTRA was founded to maintain the standards of work conditions and wages for professional singers, narrators, and sound-effects engineers. Like its sister union, the American Federation of Musicians, AFTRA protects the rights of its members with regard to wages and working conditions.

## Selected Bibliography

BLUES

1.  Charters, Sam. *The Bluesmen.* Oak Publications, New York, 1972.
2.  Guralnick, Peter. *Feel like Going Home.* Omnibus, London, 1979.

COUNTRY AND WESTERN

1.  Horstman, Dorothy. *Sing Your Heart Out, Country Boy.* Dutton, New York, 1975.
2.  Malone, William C. *Country Music, USA.* University Press, Austin, Texas, 1970.
3.  Shelton, Robert. *The Country Music Story.* Castle Books, New Jersey, 1971.
4.  Wacholta, Larry E. *Inside Country Music.* Billboard Publications, Inc., New York, 1986.
5.  Whitburn, Joel. *Top Country 1945-1985.* Billboard Publications, Inc., New York, 1985.

JAZZ

1.  Baker, David. *Jazz Improvisation.* Maher Publications, Chicago, 1969.
2.  Coker, Jerry, Jimmy Casale, Gary Campbell, and Jerry Greene. *Patterns for Jazz.* Studio P.R., Inc., Lebanon, Indiana, 1970.
3.  Collier, James Lincoln. *The Making of Jazz: A Comprehensive History.* Dell Publishing Co., Inc., New York, 1979.
4.  Feather, Leonard. *The Encyclopedia of Jazz.* Quartet Books, London, 1984.

MIDI

1.  Boom, Michael. *Music Through Midi.* Microsoft Press, Washington, 1987.
2.  Massey, Howard and the Staff of CEM. *The Complete Guide to MIDI Software.* Amsco Publications, New York, 1986.

THE MUSIC BUSINESS

1.  Csida, Joseph. *The Music/Record Career Handbook.* Billboard Publications, Inc., New York, 1980.
2.  Feist, Leonard, *An Introduction to Popular Music Publishing in America.* National Music Publishers' Association, Inc., New York, 1980.
3.  Shemel, Sidney and M. William Krasilovsky. *This Business of Music, Fifth Edition, Revised and Enlarged: Including the Latest Copyright and Tax Information, Updated Forms, and an All New Section on Video Rights.* Billboard Publications, Inc., New York, 1985.
4.  Shemel, Sidney and M. William Krasilovsky. *More About This Business of Music, Third Edition, Revised and Enlarged.* Billboard Publications, Inc., New York, 1982.

MUSIC THEORY AND ARRANGING

1.  Forte, Allen. *Tonal Harmony in Concept and Practice.* Holt, Rinehart and Winston, Inc., New York, 1974.

2. Persichetti, Vincent. *Twentieth Century Harmony.* W.W. Norton and Company, New York, 1961.
3. Sebesky, Don. *The Contemporary Arranger.* Alfred Music Publishers, 1975.

## POP

1. Bronson, Fred. *The Billboard Book of #1 Hits.* Billboard Publications, Inc., New York, 1985.
2. Goldberg, Isaac. *Tin Pan Alley.* Ungar, New York, 1961.
3. Whitburn, Joel. *The Billboard Book of Top 40 Hits.* 3rd Ed., Billboard Publications, Inc., New York, 1987.
4. Wilder, Alec. *American Popular Song, The Great Innovators, 1900-1950.* Edited and with an introduction by James T. Maher, Oxford University Press, London, Oxford, New York, 1972.

## RECORDING

1. Anderton, Craig. *Home Recording for Musicians.* Amsco Publications, New York, 1978.
2. Miller, Fred. *Studio Recording for Musicians.* Amsco Publications, New York, 1981.

## ROCK AND ROLL

1. Escott, Colin and Martin Hawkins. *Sun Records: The Brief History of the Legendary Record Label.* Quick Fox, New York, 1980.
2. Gillett, Charles. *The Sound of the City.* Pantheon Books, New York, 1983.
3. Ward, Ed, Geoffrey Stokes & Ken Tucker. *Rock of Ages, The Rolling Stone History of Rock & Roll.* Rolling Stone Press/Summit Books, New York, 1986.

## SONG LYRICS

1. David, Sheila. *The Craft of Lyric Writing.* Writer's Digest Books, Cincinnati, 1985.
2. Goldstein, Richard. *The Poetry of Rock.* Bantam, New York, 1969.
3. Morris, William and Mary. *Harper Dictionary of Contemporary Usage.* Harper & Row, Publishers, New York, 1985.
4. *The Chicago Manual of Style,* The University of Chicago Press, Chicago, 1982.
5. Wentworth and Flexner. *Dictionary of American Slang.* T.Y. Crowell, New York, 1975.

## SOUL AND RHYTHM AND BLUES

1. Garland, Phyl. *The Sound of Soul.* Regnery, Chicago, 1969.
2. Whitburn, Joel. *Top Black: 1942-1985.* Billboard Publications, Inc., New York, 1985.

# Index

## Permissions continued

"Nasty" Words and Music by James Harris III and Terry Lewis. Copyright 1986 FLYTE TIME TUNES (ASCAP). All Rights Reserved. International Copyright Secured. Used by Permission. Excerpted on page 148.

"Superfly" by Curtis Mayfield. © 1972 WARNER-TAMERLANE PUBLISHING CORP. All Rights Reserved. Used by Permission. Excerpted on page 69.

"Freddie's Dead" by Curtis Mayfield. © 1972 CURTOM PUBLISHING CO., INC. All Rights Reserved. Used by Permission. Excerpted on page 70.

"Anything Goes" by Cole Porter. © 1934 WARNER BROS., INC. (Renewed). All Rights Reserved. Used by Permission. Excerpted on page 133.

"Lookin' for Love" Words and music by Wanda Mallette, Patti Ryan, and Bob Morrison. © 1979 Southern Nights Music, 35 Music Square East, Nashville, TN 37203. International Copyright Secured. Used by Permission. Excerpted on page 23.

"All for the Best" by Stephen Schwartz. Copyright © 1971 by Range Road Music, Quartet Music, and New Cadenza Music. Excerpted on page 133.

Quotes on pages 12, 15, 20, 46, 78, 92, 94, 95, 96, 115, and 178 Reprinted by Permission of Cherry Lane Music Co., Inc., from *Interviews with Great Contemporary Songwriters* by Brian Pollock.